Ben Stacy Jerrik (Ed.)

Graph Database

Ben Stacy Jerrik (Ed.)

Graph Database

Graph (abstract data type), Database, Computer data storage

Part Press

Contents

Articles

References

Graph_database

A **graph database** uses graph structures with nodes, edges, and properties to represent and store data. By definition, a graph database is any storage system that provides index-free adjacency. This means that every element contains a direct pointer to its adjacent element and no index lookups are necessary. General graph databases that can store any graph are distinct from specialized graph databases such as triplestores and network databases.

Structure

Graph databases are based on graph theory. Graph databases employ nodes, properties, and edges. Nodes are very similar in nature to the objects that object-oriented programmers will be familiar with.

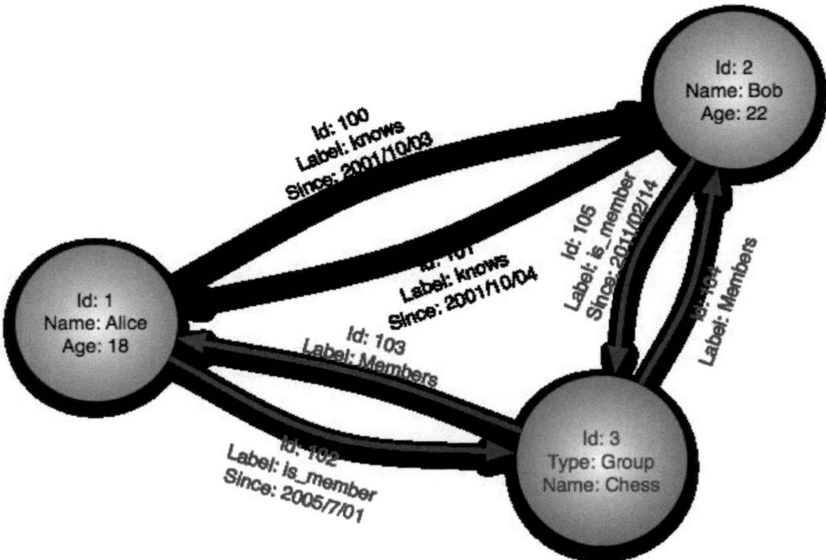

Nodes represent entities such as people, businesses, accounts, or any other item you might want to keep track of.

Properties are pertinent information that relate to nodes. For instance, if "Wikipedia" were one of the nodes, one might have it tied to properties such as "website", "reference material", or "word that starts with the letter 'w'", depending on which aspects of "Wikipedia" are pertinent to the particular database.

Edges are the lines that connect nodes to nodes or nodes to properties and they represent the relationship between the two. Most of the important information is really stored in the edges. Meaningful patterns emerge when one examines the connections and interconnections of nodes, properties, and edges.

Properties

Compared with relational databases, graph databases are often faster for associative data sets, and map more directly to the structure of object-oriented applications. They can scale more naturally to large data sets as they do not typically require expensive join operations. As they depend less on a rigid schema, they are more suitable to manage ad-hoc and changing data with evolving schemas. Conversely, relational databases are typically faster at performing the same operation on large numbers of data elements.

Graph databases are a powerful tool for graph-like queries, for example computing the shortest path between two nodes in the graph. Other graph-like queries can be performed over a graph database in a natural way (for example graph's diameter computations or community detection).

Graph database projects

The following is a list of several well-known graph database projects:[1]

- AllegroGraph - a scalable, high-performance RDF and graph database.
- Bigdata [2] - a highly scalable RDF/graph database capable of 10B+ edges on a single node or clustered deployment for very high throughput.
- CloudGraph [3] - a disk- and memory-based, fully transactional .NET graph database that uses graphs and key/value pairs to store data.
- Cytoscape - open-source platform, outgrowth of bioinformatics
- DEX[4] - A high-performance graph database from Sparsity Technologies [5], a technology transition company from DAMA-UPC [6]
- Filament [7] - graph persistence framework and associated toolkits based on a navigational query style.
- GiraffeDB [8] - a powerful graph database system for the .NET framework 4.0, capable of representing complex semantics in an efficient and accessible way.
- GraphBase [9] - a customizable, distributed, small-footprint, high-performance graph store with a rich tool set from FactNexus [10]
- Graphd, the proprietary backend of Freebase
- Horton [11] - a graph database from Microsoft Research Extreme Computing Group (XCG) [12] based on the cloud programming infrastructure Orleans [13]
- HyperGraphDB [14] - an open-source (LGPL) graph database supporting generalized hypergraphs where edges can point to other edges
- InfiniteGraph [15] - a highly scalable, distributed and cloud-enabled commercial product with flexible licensing for startups.
- InfoGrid [16] - an open-source / commercial (AGPLv3, free for small entities)[17] graph database with web front end and configurable storage engines (MySQL, PostgreSQL, Files, Hadoop)
- Neo4j - an open-source / commercial (GPLv3 community edition, AGPLv3 advanced and enterprise edition)[18] graph database
- OpenLink Virtuoso - a high performance RDF graph database server, deployable as a local embedded instance (as used in the Nepomuk Semantic Desktop), a single-instance network server, or a massively scalable shared-nothing network cluster instance.
- OrientDB - a high-performance open source document-graph database
- OQGRAPH [19] - Graph computation engine (GPLv2 licensed) for MySQL, MariaDB and Drizzle
- R2DF [20] - R2DF framework for ranked path queries over weighted RDF graphs
- sones GraphDB - an open-source / commercial (AGPLv3)[21] graph database and universal access layer (funded by Deutsche Telekom AG)
- VertexDB [22] - high performance graph database server that supports automatic garbage collection.

Distributed Graph Processing (mostly in-memory-only)

- Angrapa [23] - graph package in Hama [24], a bulk synchronous parallel (BSP) platform
- Apache Hama [24] - a pure BSP(Bulk Synchronous Parallel) computing framework on top of HDFS (Hadoop Distributed File System) for massive scientific computations such as matrix, graph and network algorithms.
- Bigdata [2] - a highly scalable RDF/graph database capable of 10B+ edges on a single node or clustered deployment for very high throughput.
- FlockDB - an open source distributed, fault-tolerant graph database based on MySQL and the Gizzard framework for managing Twitter-like graph data (single-hop relationships) at webscale FlockDB on GitHub [25].
- Giraph [26] - a Graph processing infrastructure that runs on Hadoop (see Pregel).
- GoldenOrb [27] - Pregel implementation built on top of Apache Hadoop
- HipG [28] - a library for high-level parallel processing of large-scale graphs. HipG is implemented in Java and is designed for distributed-memory machine
- JPregel [29] - In-memory java based Pregel implementation
- KDT [30] - An open-source distributed graph library with a Python front-end and C++/MPI backend (Combinatorial BLAS [31]).
- OpenLink Virtuoso - the shared-nothing Cluster Edition enables massively scalable and distributable graph data processing.
- Phoebus [32] - Pregel implementation written in Erlang
- Pregel [33] - Google's internal graph processing platform, released details in ACM paper.
- Signal/Collect [34] - a framework for parallel graph processing written in Scala
- Trinity [35] - Distributed in-memory graph engine under development at Microsoft Research Labs.

APIs and Graph Query/Programming Languages

- Blueprints [36] - a Java API for Property Graphs from TinkerPop [37] and supported by a few graph database vendors.
- Blueprints.NET [38] - a C#/.NET API for generic Property Graphs.
- Bulbflow [39] - a Python persistence framework for Rexster and Neo4j Server.
- Cypher [40] - a Property Graph Query Language developed by Neo4j.
- Gremlin [41] - an open-source graph programming language that works over various graph database systems.
- Pacer [42] - is a Ruby dialect/implementation of the Gremlin graph traversal language.
- Pipes [43] - a lazy dataflow framework written in Java that forms the foundation for various property graph traversal languages.
- PYBlueprints [44] - a Python API for Property Graphs.
- Rexster [45] - a HTTP/REST API for accessing remote graph databases and supported by a few graph database vendors.
- SPARQL - an extension of the SQL standard, allowing execution of SPARQL queries within SQL statements, typically by treating them as subquery or function clauses. This also allows SPARQL queries to be issued through "traditional" data access APIs (ODBC, JDBC, OLE DB, ADO.NET, etc.)
- SPASQL [46] - an extension of the SQL standard, allowing execution of SPARQL queries within SQL statements, typically by treating them as subquery or function clauses. This also allows SPARQL queries to be issued through "traditional" data access APIs (ODBC, JDBC, OLE DB, ADO.NET, etc.)
- Styx [47] - (previously named Pipes.Net) a data flow framework for C#/.NET for processing generic graphs and Property Graphs.

See also

- NoSQL (concept)
- Document-oriented database
- Structured storage
- Object database
- Resource Description Framework (RDF) - framework to express node-edge graphs
- Graph transformation for a complementary topic (rule based in memory manipulation of graphs instead of transaction safe persistence).
- RDF Database

References

[1] http://graph-database.org

[2] http://www.bigdata.com/blog

[3] http://www.cloudgraph.com

[4] http://sparsity-technologies.com/dex

[5] http://sparsity-technologies.com

[6] http://www.dama.upc.edu/technology-transfer/dex

[7] http://filament.sourceforge.net/

[8] http://www.giraffedb.net/

[9] http://graphbase.net/

[10] http://factnexus.com/

[11] http://research.microsoft.com/en-us/projects/ldg

[12] http://research.microsoft.com/en-us/labs/xcg

[13] http://research.microsoft.com/en-us/projects/orleans/default.aspx

[14] http://www.hypergraphdb.org

[15] http://infinitegraph.com

[16] http://infogrid.org/

[17] http://infogrid.org/wiki/Docs/License

[18] http://neotechnology.com/products

[19] http://openquery.com/graph

[20] http://dl.acm.org/citation.cfm?id=1988736/

[21] http://sones.com/

[22] http://www.dekorte.com/projects/opensource/vertexdb/

[23] http://wiki.apache.org/hama/GraphPackage

[24] http://incubator.apache.org/hama/

[25] https://github.com/twitter/flockdb

[26] http://github.com/aching/Giraph

[27] http://www.goldenorbos.org

[28] http://www.cs.vu.nl/~ekr/hipg/

[29] http://kowshik.github.com/JPregel/

[30] http://kdt.sourceforge.net

[31] http://gauss.cs.ucsb.edu/~aydin/CombBLAS/html/index.html

[32] http://github.com/xslogic/phoebus

[33] http://portal.acm.org/citation.cfm?id=1582723

[34] http://code.google.com/p/signal-collect/

[35] http://research.microsoft.com/en-us/projects/trinity/

[36] http://blueprints.tinkerpop.com

[37] http://www.tinkerpop.com/

[38] http://github.com/ahzf/blueprints.NET

[39] http://bulbflow.com

[40] http://docs.neo4j.org/chunked/snapshot/cypher-query-lang.html

[41] http://gremlin.tinkerpop.com/

[42] http://github.com/pangloss/pacer

[43] http://pipes.tinkerpop.com

[44] http://pypi.python.org/pypi/pyblueprints/0.1

[45] http://rexster.tinkerpop.com
[46] http://www.w3.org/wiki/SPASQL
[47] https://github.com/ahzf/Styx

External links

- Graph Database Tutorial (http://infogrid.org/blog/2010/02/operations-on-a-graph-database-part-1/)
- NoSQL Frankfurt 2010 - The GraphDB Landscape and sones (http://www.slideshare.net/ahzf/nosql-frankfurt-2010-the-graphdb-landscape-and-sones)
- Graph Databases and the Future of Large-Scale Knowledge Management (http://highscalability.com/paper-graph-databases-and-future-large-scale-knowledge-management)
- Graphs in the database: SQL meets social networks (http://techportal.ibuildings.com/2009/09/07/graphs-in-the-database-sql-meets-social-networks/)
- Social networks in the database: using a graph database (http://blog.neo4j.org/2009/09/social-networks-in-database-using-graph.html)
- Scaling Online Social Networks without Pains (http://netdb09.cis.upenn.edu/netdb09papers/netdb09-final3.pdf)
- Large-scale Graph Computing at Google (http://highscalability.com/blog/2009/6/15/large-scale-graph-computing-at-google.html)
- On building a stupidly fast graph database (http://blog.directededge.com/2009/02/27/on-building-a-stupidly-fast-graph-database/)
- InfiniteGraph technical documentation (http://www.infinitegraph.com/information/index.html#docs)
- Neo4j - an open source graph database (http://neo4j.org/)
- DEX - a high-performance graph database (http://www.sparsity-technologies.com/dex)
- Eric Lai. (2009, July 1). No to SQL? Anti-database movement gains steam (http://www.computerworld.com/s/article/9135086/No_to_SQL_Anti_database_movement_gains_steam_)
- Renzo Angles, Claudio Gutierrez. Survey of graph database models (http://portal.acm.org/citation.cfm?id=1322433). ACM Computing Surveys, Feb. 2008.
- InfoGrid (http://infogrid.org/) - an open-source application platform including a graph database
- Rodriguez, M.A., MySQL vs. Neo4j on a Large-Scale Graph Traversal (http://markorodriguez.com/2011/02/18/mysql-vs-neo4j-on-a-large-scale-graph-traversal/)
- Rodriguez, M.A., Neubauer, P, The Graph Traversal Pattern (http://arxiv.org/abs/1004.1001) article.
- OrientDB - a high-performance open source document-graph database (http://www.orientechnologies.com/)
- Optimizing Schema-Last Tuple-Store Queries in Graphd (http://portal.acm.org/citation.cfm?id=1807283) SIGMOD 2010

Graph_(abstract_data_type)

In computer science, a **graph** is an abstract data type that is meant to implement the graph and hypergraph concepts from mathematics.

A graph data structure consists of a finite (and possibly mutable) set of ordered pairs, called **edges** or **arcs**, of certain entities called **nodes** or **vertices**. As in mathematics, an edge (x,y) is said to **point** or **go from** x to y. The nodes may be part of the graph structure, or may be external entities represented by integer indices or references.

A graph data structure may also associate to each edge some **edge value**, such as a symbolic label or a numeric attribute (cost, capacity, length, etc.).

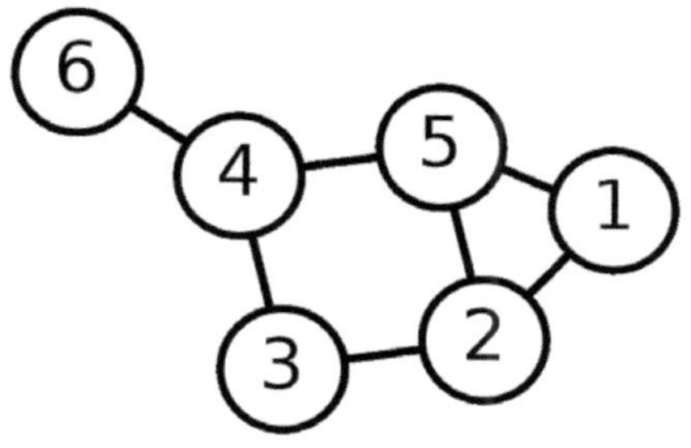

A labeled graph of 6 vertices and 7 edges.

Algorithms

Graph algorithms are a significant field of interest within computer science. Typical higher-level operations associated with graphs are: finding a path between two nodes, like depth-first search and breadth-first search and finding the shortest path from one node to another, like Dijkstra's algorithm. A solution to finding the shortest path from each node to every other node also exists in the form of the Floyd–Warshall algorithm.

A directed graph can be seen as a flow network, where each edge has a capacity and each edge receives a flow. The Ford–Fulkerson algorithm is used to find out the maximum flow from a source to a sink in a graph.

Operations

The basic operations provided by a graph data structure G usually include:

- adjacent(G, x, y): tests whether there is an edge from node x to node y.
- neighbors(G, x): lists all nodes y such that there is an edge from x to y.
- add(G, x, y): adds to G the edge from x to y, if it is not there.
- delete(G, x, y): removes the edge from x to y, if it is there.
- get_node_value(G, x): returns the value associated with the node x.
- set_node_value(G, x, a): sets the value associated with the node x to a.

Structures that associate values to the edges usually also provide:

- get_edge_value(G, x, y): returns the value associated to the edge (x,y).
- set_edge_value(G, x, y, v): sets the value associated to the edge (x,y) to v.

Representations

Different data structures for the representation of graphs are used in practice:

- **Adjacency list** – Vertices are stored as records or objects, and every vertex stores a list of adjacent vertices. This data structure allows the storage of additional data on the vertices.
- **Incidence list** – Vertices and edges are stored as records or objects. Each vertex stores its incident edges, and each edge stores its incident vertices. This data structure allows the storage of additional data on vertices and edges.
- **Adjacency matrix** – A two-dimensional matrix, in which the rows represent source vertices and columns represent destination vertices. Data on edges and vertices must be stored externally. Only the cost for one edge can be stored between each pair of vertices.
- **Incidence matrix** – A two-dimensional Boolean matrix, in which the rows represent the vertices and columns represent the edges. The entries indicate whether the vertex at a row is incident to the edge at a column.

The following table gives the time complexity cost of performing various operations on graphs, for each of these representations. In the matrix representations, the entries encode the cost of following an edge. The cost of edges that are not present are assumed to be .

	Adjacency list	Incidence list	Adjacency matrix	Incidence matrix
Storage				
Add vertex				
Add edge				
Remove vertex				
Remove edge				
Query: are vertices u, v adjacent? (Assuming that the storage positions for u, v are known)				
Remarks	When removing edges or vertices, need to find all vertices or edges		Slow to add or remove vertices, because matrix must be resized/copied	Slow to add or remove vertices and edges, because matrix must be resized/copied

Adjacency lists are generally preferred because they efficiently represent sparse graphs. An adjacency matrix is preferred if the graph is dense, that is the number of edges E is close to the number of vertices squared, V^2, or if one must be able to quickly look up if there is an edge connecting two vertices.[1]

Types

- Skip graphs

See also

- Graph traversal for graph walking strategies
- Graph database for graph (data structure) persistency
- Graph rewriting for rule based transformations of graphs (graph data structures)
- GraphStream
- Graphviz
- yEd Graph Editor – Java-based diagram editor for creating and editing graphs

References

[1] Cormen, Thomas H.; Leiserson, Charles E.; Rivest, Ronald L.; Stein, Clifford (2001). Introduction to Algorithms (2nd ed.). MIT Press and McGraw–Hill. ISBN 0-262-53196-8.

Further reading

- "18: Graph Data Structures" (http://hamilton.bell.ac.uk/swdev2/notes/notes_18.pdf). *Software Development 2*. Bell College.

External links

- Boost Graph Library: a powerful C++ graph library (http://www.boost.org/libs/graph)

Database

A **database** is an organized collection of data, today typically in digital form. The data are typically organized to model relevant aspects of reality (for example, the availability of rooms in hotels), in a way that supports processes requiring this information (for example, finding a hotel with vacancies).

The term *database* is correctly applied to the data and their supporting data structures, and not to the database management system (DBMS). The database data collection with DBMS is called a database system.

The term *database system* implies that the data is managed to some level of quality (measured in terms of accuracy, availability, usability, and resilience) and this in turn often implies the use of a general-purpose database management system (DBMS).[1] A general-purpose DBMS is typically a complex software system that meets many usage requirements, and the databases that it maintains are often large and complex. The utilization of databases is now spread to such a wide degree that virtually every technology and product relies on databases and DBMSs for its development and commercialization, or even may have such embedded in it. Also, organizations and companies, from small to large, heavily depend on databases for their operations.

Well known DBMSs include Oracle, IBM DB2, Microsoft SQL Server, Microsoft Access, PostgreSQL, MySQL, and SQLite. A database is not generally portable across different DBMS, but different DBMSs can inter-operate to some degree by using standards like SQL and ODBC to support together a single application. A DBMS also needs to provide effective run-time execution to properly support (e.g., in terms of performance, availability, and security) as many end-users as needed.

A way to classify databases involves the type of their contents, for example: bibliographic, document-text, statistical, or multimedia objects. Another way is by their application area, for example: accounting, music compositions, movies, banking, manufacturing, or insurance.

The term *database* may be narrowed to specify particular aspects of organized collection of data and may refer to the logical database, to physical database as data content in computer data storage or to many other database sub-definitions.

History

Database concept

The database concept has evolved since the 1960s to ease increasing difficulties in designing, building, and maintaining complex information systems (typically with many concurrent end-users, and with a large amount of diverse data). It has evolved together with database management systems which enable the effective handling of databases. Though the terms database and DBMS define different entities, they are inseparable: a database's properties are determined by its supporting DBMS and vice-versa. The Oxford English dictionary cites a 1962 technical report as the first to use the term "data-base." With the progress in technology in the areas of processors, computer memory, computer storage and computer networks, the sizes, capabilities, and performance of databases and their respective DBMSs have grown in orders of magnitudes. For decades it has been unlikely that a complex information system can be built effectively without a proper database supported by a DBMS. The utilization of databases is now spread to such a wide degree that virtually every technology and product relies on databases and DBMSs for its development and commercialization, or even may have such embedded in it. Also, organizations and companies, from small to large, heavily depend on databases for their operations.

No widely accepted exact definition exists for DBMS. However, a system needs to provide considerable functionality to qualify as a DBMS. Accordingly its supported data collection needs to meet respective usability requirements (broadly defined by the requirements below) to qualify as a database. Thus, a database and its supporting DBMS are defined here by a set of general requirements listed below. Virtually all existing mature DBMS products meet these requirements to a great extent, while less mature either meet them or converge to meet them.

Evolution of database and DBMS technology

See also *Database management system#History*

The introduction of the term *database* coincided with the availability of direct-access storage (disks and drums) from the mid-1960s onwards. The term represented a contrast with the tape-based systems of the past, allowing shared interactive use rather than daily batch processing.

In the earliest database systems, efficiency was perhaps the primary concern, but it was already recognized that there were other important objectives. One of the key aims was to make the data independent of the logic of application programs, so that the same data could be made available to different applications.

The first generation of database systems were *navigational*,[2] applications typically accessed data by following pointers from one record to another. The two main data models at this time were the hierarchical model, epitomized by IBM's IMS system, and the Codasyl model (Network model), implemented in a number of products such as IDMS.

The Relational model, first proposed in 1970 by Edgar F. Codd, departed from this tradition by insisting that applications should search for data by content, rather than by following links. This was considered necessary to allow the content of the database to evolve without constant rewriting of applications. Relational systems placed heavy demands on processing resources, and it was not until the mid 1980s that computing hardware became powerful enough to allow them to be widely deployed. By the early 1990s, however, relational systems were dominant for all large-scale data processing applications, and they remain dominant today (2012) except in niche areas. The dominant database language is the standard SQL for the Relational model, which has influenced database languages also for other data models.

Because the relational model emphasizes search rather than navigation, it does not make relationships between different entities explicit in the form of pointers, but represents them rather using *primary keys* and *foreign keys*. While this is a good basis for a query language, it is less well suited as a modeling language. For this reason a different model, the Entity-relationship model which emerged shortly later (1976), gained popularity for database design.

In the period since the 1970s database technology has kept pace with the increasing resources becoming available from the computing platform: notably the rapid increase in the capacity and speed (and reduction in price) of disk storage, and the increasing capacity of main memory. This has enabled ever larger databases and higher throughputs to be achieved.

The rigidity of the relational model, in which all data is held in tables with a fixed structure of rows and columns, has increasingly been seen as a limitation when handling information that is richer or more varied in structure than the traditional 'ledger-book' data of corporate information systems: for example, document databases, engineering databases, multimedia databases, or databases used in the molecular sciences. Various attempts have been made to address this problem, many of them gathering under banners such as *post-relational* or *NoSQL*. Two developments of note are the Object database and the XML database. The vendors of relational databases have fought off competition from these newer models by extending the capabilities of their own products to support a wider variety of data types.

General-purpose DBMS

A DBMS has evolved into a complex software system and its development typically requires thousands of person-years of development effort. Some general-purpose DBMSs, like Oracle, Microsoft SQL Server, and IBM DB2, have been undergoing upgrades for thirty years or more. General-purpose DBMSs aim to satisfy as many applications as possible, which typically makes them even more complex than special-purpose databases. However, the fact that they can be used "off the shelf", as well as their amortized cost over many applications and instances, makes them an attractive alternative (Vs. one-time development) whenever they meet an application's requirements.

Though attractive in many cases, a general-purpose DBMS is not always the optimal solution: When certain applications are pervasive with many operating instances, each with many users, a general-purpose DBMS may introduce unnecessary overhead and too large "footprint" (too large amount of unnecessary, unutilized software code). Such applications usually justify dedicated development. Typical examples are email systems, though they need to possess certain DBMS properties: email systems are built in a way that optimizes email messages handling and managing, and do not need significant portions of a general-purpose DBMS functionality.

Types of people involved

Three types of people are involved with a general-purpose DBMS:

1. **DBMS developers** - These are the people that design and build the DBMS product, and the only ones who touch its code. They are typically the employees of a DBMS vendor (e.g., Oracle, IBM, Microsoft, Sybase), or, in the case of Open source DBMSs (e.g., MySQL), volunteers or people supported by interested companies and organizations. They are typically skilled systems programmers. DBMS development is a complicated task, and some of the popular DBMSs have been under development and enhancement (also to follow progress in technology) for decades.
2. **Application developers** and **Database administrators** - These are the people that design and build a database-based application that uses the DBMS. The latter group members design the needed database and maintain it. The first group members write the needed application programs which the application comprises. Both are well familiar with the DBMS product and use its user interfaces (as well as usually other tools) for their work. Sometimes the application itself is packaged and sold as a separate product, which may include the DBMS inside (see Embedded database; subject to proper DBMS licensing), or sold separately as an add-on to the DBMS.
3. **Application's end-users** (e.g., accountants, insurance people, medical doctors, etc.) - These people know the application and its end-user interfaces, but need not know nor understand the underlying DBMS. Thus, though they are the intended and main beneficiaries of a DBMS, they are only indirectly involved with it.

Database machines and appliances

In the 1970s and 1980s attempts were made to build database systems with integrated hardware and software. The underlying philosophy was that such integration would provide higher performance at lower cost. Examples were IBM System/38, the early offering of Teradata, and the Britton Lee, Inc. database machine. Another approach to hardware support for database management was ICL's CAFS accelerator, a hardware disk controller with programmable search capabilities. In the long term these efforts were generally unsuccessful because specialized database machines could not keep pace with the rapid development and progress of general-purpose computers. Thus most database systems nowadays are software systems running on general-purpose hardware, using general-purpose computer data storage. However this idea is still pursued for certain applications by some companies like Netezza and Oracle (Exadata).

Database research

Database research has been an active and diverse area, with many specializations, carried out since the early days of dealing with the database concept in the 1960s. It has strong ties with database technology and DBMS products. Database research has taken place at research and development groups of companies (e.g., notably at IBM Research, who contributed technologies and ideas virtually to any DBMS existing today), research institutes, and Academia. Research has been done both through Theory and Prototypes. The interaction between research and database related product development has been very productive to the database area, and many related key concepts and technologies emerged from it. Notable are the Relational and the Entity-relationship models, the Atomic transaction concept and related Concurrency control techniques, Query languages and Query optimization methods, RAID, and more. Research has provided deep insight to virtually all aspects of databases, though not always has been pragmatic, effective (and cannot and should not always be: research is exploratory in nature, and not always leads to accepted or useful ideas). Ultimately market forces and real needs determine the selection of problem solutions and related technologies, also among those proposed by research. However, occasionally, not the best and most elegant solution wins (e.g., SQL). Along their history DBMSs and respective databases, to a great extent, have been the outcome of such research, while real product requirements and challenges triggered database research directions and sub-areas.

The database research area has several notable dedicated academic journals (e.g., ACM Transactions on Database Systems-TODS, Data and Knowledge Engineering-DKE, and more) and annual conferences (e.g., ACM SIGMOD, ACM PODS, VLDB, IEEE ICDE, and more), as well as an active and quite heterogeneous (subject-wise) research community all over the world.

Database type examples

The following are examples of various database types. Some of them are not main-stream types, but most of them have received special attention (e.g., in research) due to end-user requirements. Some exist as specialized DBMS products, and some have their functionality types incorporated in existing general-purpose DBMSs.

- **Active database**

    An *active database* is a database that includes an event-driven architecture which can respond to conditions both inside and outside the database. Possible uses include security monitoring, alerting, statistics gathering and authorization.

    Most modern relational databases include active database features in the form of database trigger.

- **Cloud database**

    A *Cloud database* is a database that relies on cloud technology. Both the database and most of its DBMS reside remotely, "in the cloud," while its applications are both developed by programmers and later maintained and utilized by (application's) end-users through a Web browser and Open APIs. More and more such database products are emerging, both of new vendors and by virtually all established database vendors.

- **Data warehouse**

    Data warehouses archive data from operational databases and often from external sources such as market research firms. Often operational data undergoes transformation on its way into the warehouse, getting summarized, anonymized, reclassified, etc. The warehouse becomes the central source of data for use by managers and other end-users who may not have access to operational data. For example, sales data might be aggregated to weekly totals and converted from internal product codes to use UPCs so that it can be compared with ACNielsen data. Some basic and essential components of data warehousing include retrieving, analyzing, and mining data, transforming,loading and managing data so as to make it available for further use.

Operations in a data warehouse are typically concerned with bulk data manipulation, and as such, it is unusual and inefficient to target individual rows for update, insert or delete. Bulk native loaders for input data and bulk SQL passes for aggregation are the norm.

- **Distributed database**

  The definition of a *distributed database* is broad, and may be utilized in different meanings. In general it typically refers to a modular DBMS architecture that allows distinct DBMS instances to cooperate as a single DBMS over processes, computers, and sites, while managing a single database distributed itself over multiple computers, and different sites.

  Examples are databases of local work-groups and departments at regional offices, branch offices, manufacturing plants and other work sites. These databases can include both segments shared by multiple sites, and segments specific to one site and used only locally in that site.

- **Document-oriented database**

  Utilized to conveniently store, manage, edit and retrieve documents.

- **Embedded database**

  An *embedded database* system is a DBMS which is tightly integrated with an application software that requires access to stored data in a way that the DBMS is "hidden" from the application's end-user and requires little or no ongoing maintenance. It is actually a broad technology category that includes DBMSs with differing properties and target markets. The term "embedded database" can be confusing because only a small subset of embedded database products is used in real-time embedded systems such as telecommunications switches and consumer electronics devices.[3]

- **End-user database**

  These databases consist of data developed by individual end-users. Examples of these are collections of documents, spreadsheets, presentations, multimedia, and other files. Several products exist to support such databases. Some of them are much simpler than full fledged DBMSs, with more elementary DBMS functionality (e.g., not supporting multiple concurrent end-users on a same database), with basic programming interfaces, and a relatively small "foot-print" (not much code to run as in "regular" general-purpose databases). However, also available general-purpose DBMSs can often be used for such purpose, if they provide basic user-interfaces for straightforward database applications (limited query and data display; no real programming needed), while still enjoying the database qualities and protections that these DBMSs can provide.

- **Federated database and multi-database**

  A *federated database* is an integrated database that comprises several distinct databases, each with its own DBMS. It is handled as a single database by a federated database management system (FDBMS), which transparently integrates multiple autonomous DBMSs, possibly of different types (which makes it a heterogeneous database), and provides them with an integrated conceptual view. The constituent databases are interconnected via computer network, and may be geographically decentralized.

  Sometime the term *multi-database* is used as a synonym to federated database, though it may refer to a less integrated (e.g., without an FDBMS and a managed integrated schema) group of databases that cooperate in a single application. In this case typically middleware for distribution is used which typically includes an atomic commit protocol (ACP), e.g., the two-phase commit protocol, to allow distributed (global) transactions (vs. local transactions confined to a single DBMS) across the participating databases.

- **Graph database**

  A *graph database* is a kind of NoSQL database that uses graph structures with nodes, edges, and properties to represent and store information. General graph databases that can store any graph are distinct from specialized graph databases such as triplestores and network databases.

- **Hypermedia databases**

  The World Wide Web can be thought of as a database, albeit one spread across millions of independent computing systems. Web browsers "process" this data one page at a time, while Web crawlers and other software provide the equivalent of database indexes to support search and other activities.

- **In-memory database**

  An *in-memory database* (IMDB; also *main memory database* or **MMDB**) is a database that primarily resides in main memory, but typically backed-up by non-volatile computer data storage. Main memory databases are faster than disk databases. Accessing data in memory reduces the I/O reading activity when, for example, querying the data. In applications where response time is critical, such as telecommunications network equipment, main memory databases are often used.[4]

- **Knowledge base**

  A **knowledge base** (abbreviated **KB, kb** or Δ[5] [6]) is a special kind of database for knowledge management, providing the means for the computerized collection, organization, and retrieval of knowledge. Also a collection of data representing problems with their solutions and related experiences.

- **Operational database**

  These databases store detailed data about the operations of an organization. They are typically organized by subject matter, process relatively high volumes of updates using transactions. Essentially every major organization on earth uses such databases. Examples include customer databases that record contact, credit, and demographic information about a business' customers, personnel databases that hold information such as salary, benefits, skills data about employees, Enterprise resource planning that record details about product components, parts inventory, and financial databases that keep track of the organization's money, accounting and financial dealings.

- **Parallel database**

  A **parallel database**, run by a parallel DBMS, seeks to improve performance through parallelization for tasks such as loading data, building indexes and evaluating queries. Parallel databases improve processing and input/output speeds by using multiple central processing units (CPUs) (including multi-core processors) and storage in parallel. In parallel processing, many operations are performed simultaneously, as opposed to serial, sequential processing, where operations are performed with no time overlap.

  The major parallel DBMS architectures (which are induced by the underlying hardware architecture are:

  - **Shared memory architecture**, where multiple processors share the main memory space, as well as other data storage.
  - **Shared disk architecture**, where each processing unit (typically consisting of multiple processors) has its own main memory, but all units share the other storage.
  - **Shared nothing architecture**, where each processing unit has its own main memory and other storage.

- **Real-time database**

If a DBMS system responses users' request in a given time period, it can be regarded as a real time database.

- **Spatial database**

A spatial database can store the data with multidimensional features. The queries on such data include location based queries, like "where is the closest hotel in my area".

- **Temporal database**

- **Unstructured-data database**

> An unstructured-data database is intended to store in a manageable and protected way diverse objects that do not fit naturally and conveniently in common databases. It may include email messages, documents, journals, multimedia objects etc. The name may be misleading since some objects can be highly structured. However, the entire possible object collection does not fit into a predefined structured framework. Most established DBMSs now support unstructured data in various ways, and new dedicated DBMSs are emerging.

Major database usage requirements

The major purpose of a database is to provide the information system (in its broadest sense) that utilizes it with the information the system needs according to its own requirements. A certain broad set of requirements refines this general goal. These database requirements translate to requirements for the respective DBMS, to allow conveniently building a proper database for the given application. If this goal is met by a DBMS, then the designers and builders of the specific database can concentrate on the application's aspects, and not deal with building and maintaining the underlying DBMS. Also, since a DBMS is complex and expensive to build and maintain, it is not economical to build such a new tool (DBMS) for every application. Rather it is desired to provide a flexible tool for handling databases for as many as possible given applications, i.e., a general-purpose DBMS.

Functional requirements

Certain general functional requirements need to be met in conjunction with a database. They describe what is needed to be defined in a database for any specific application.

Defining the structure of data: Data modeling and Data definition languages

The database needs to be based on a data model that is sufficiently rich to describe in the database all the needed respective application's aspects. A data definition language exists to describe the databases within the data model. Such language is typically data model specific.

Manipulating the data: Data manipulation languages and Query languages

A database data model needs support by a sufficiently rich data manipulation language to allow all database manipulations and information generation (from the data) as needed by the respective application. Such language is typically data model specific.

Protecting the data: Setting database security types and levels

The DB needs built-in security means to protect its content (and users) from dangers of unauthorized users (either humans or programs). Protection is also provided from types of unintentional breach. Security types and levels should be defined by the database owners.

Describing processes that use the data: Workflow and Business process modeling

Manipulating database data often involves processes of several interdependent steps, at different times (e.g., when different people's interactions are involved; e.g., generating an insurance policy). Data manipulation languages are typically intended to describe what is needed in a single such step. Dealing with multiple steps typically requires writing quite complex programs. Most applications are programmed using common programming languages and software development tools. However the area of process description has evolved in the frameworks of *workflow* and *business processes* with supporting languages and software packages which considerably simplify the tasks. Traditionally these frameworks have been out of the scope of common DBMSs, but utilization of them has become common-place, and often they are provided as add-on's to DBMSs.

Operational requirements

Operational requirements are needed to be met by a database in order to effectively support an application when operational. Though it typically may be expected that operational requirements are automatically met by a DBMS, in fact it is not so in most of the cases: To be met substantial work of design and tuning is typically needed by database administrators. This is typically done by specific instructions/operations through special database user interfaces and tools, and thus may be viewed as secondary functional requirements (which are not less important than the primary).

Availability

A DB should maintain needed levels of availability, i.e., the DB needs to be available in a way that a user's action does not need to wait beyond a certain time range before starting executing upon the DB. Availability also relates to failure and recovery from it (see Recovery from failure and disaster below): Upon failure and during recovery normal availability changes, and special measures are needed to satisfy availability requirements.

Performance

Users' actions upon the DB should be executed within needed time ranges.

Isolation between users

When multiple users access the database concurrently the actions of a user should be uninterrupted and unaffected by actions of other users. These concurrent actions should maintain the DB's consistency (i.e., keep the DB from corruption).

Recovery from failure and disaster

All computer systems, including DBMSs, are prone to failures for many reasons (both software and hardware related). Failures typically corrupt the DB, typically to the extent that it is impossible to repair it without special measures. The DBMS should provide automatic recovery from failure procedures that repair the DB and return it to a well defined state.

Backup and restore

Sometimes it is desired to bring a database back to a previous state (for many reasons, e.g., cases when the database is found corrupted due to a software error, or if it has been updated with erroneous data). To achieve this a **backup** operation is done occasionally or continuously, where each desired database state (i.e., the values of its data and their embedding in database's data structures) is kept within dedicated backup files (many techniques exist to do this effectively). When this state is needed, i.e., when it is decided by a database administrator to bring the database back to this state (e.g., by specifying this state by a desired point in time when the database was in this state), these files are utilized to **restore** that state.

Data independence

Data independence pertains to a database's life cycle (see Database building, maintaining, and tuning below). It strongly impacts the convenience and cost of maintaining an application and its database, and has been the major motivation for the emergence and success of the Relational model, as well as the convergence to a common database architecture. In general the term "data independence" means that changes in the database's structure do not require changes in its application's computer programs, and that changes in the database at a certain architectural level (see below) do not affect the database's levels above. Data independence is achieved to a great extent in contemporary

DBMS, but it is not completely attainable, and achieved at different degrees for different types of database structural changes.

Major database functional areas

The functional areas are domains and subjects that have evolved in order to provide proper answers and solutions to the functional requirements above.

Data models

A data model is an abstract structure that provides the means to effectively describe specific data structures needed to model an application. As such a data model needs sufficient expressive power to capture the needed aspects of applications. These applications are often typical to commercial companies and other organizations (like manufacturing, human-resources, stock, banking, etc.). For effective utilization and handling it is desired that a data model is relatively simple and intuitive. This may be in conflict with high expressive power needed to deal with certain complex applications. Thus any popular general-purpose data model usually well balances between being intuitive and relatively simple, and very complex with high expressive power. The application's semantics is usually not explicitly expressed in the model, but rather implicit (and detailed by documentation external to the model) and hinted to by data item types' names (e.g., "part-number") and their connections (as expressed by generic data structure types provided by each specific model).

Early data models

These models were popular in the 1960s, 1970s, but nowadays can be found primarily in old legacy systems. They are characterized primarily by being navigational with strong connections between their logical and physical representations, and deficiencies in data independence.

Hierarchical model

In the Hierarchical model different record types (representing real-world entities) are embedded in a predefined hierarchical (tree-like) structure. This hierarchy is used as the physical order of records in storage. Record access is done by navigating through the data structure using pointers combined with sequential accessing.

This model has been supported primarily by the IBM IMS DBMS, one of the earliest DBMSs. Various limitations of the model have been compensated at later IMS versions by additional logical hierarchies imposed on the base physical hierarchy.

Network model

In this model a hierarchical relationship between two record types (representing real-world entities) is established by the *set* construct. A set consists of circular linked lists where one record type, the set owner or parent, appears once in each circle, and a second record type, the subordinate or child, may appear multiple times in each circle. In this way a hierarchy may be established between any two record types, e.g., type A is the owner of B. At the same time another set may be defined where B is the owner of A. Thus all the sets comprise a general directed graph (ownership defines a direction), or *network* construct. Access to records is either sequential (usually in each record type) or by navigation in the circular linked lists.

This model is more general and powerful than the hierarchical, and has been the most popular before being replaced by the Relational model. It has been standardized by CODASYL. Popular DBMS products that utilized it were Cincom Systems' Total and Cullinet's IDMS.

Inverted file model

An *inverted file* or *inverted index* of a first file, by a field in this file (the inversion field), is a second file in which this field is the key. A record in the second file includes a key and pointers to records in the first file where the inversion field has the value of the key. This is also the logical structure of contemporary database indexes. The related *Inverted file data model* utilizes inverted files of primary database files to efficiently directly access needed records in these files.

Notable for using this data model is the ADABAS DBMS of Software AG, introduced in 1970. ADABAS has gained considerable customer base and exists and supported until today. In the 1980s it has adopted the Relational model and SQL in addition to its original tools and languages.

Relational model

The relational model is a simple model that provides flexibility. It organizes data based on two-dimensional arrays known as relations, or tables as related to databases. These relations consist of a heading and a set of zero or more tuples in arbitrary order. The heading is an unordered set of zero or more attributes, or columns of the table. The tuples are a set of unique attributes mapped to values, or the rows of data in the table. Data can associated across multiple tables with a key. A key is a single, or set of multiple, attribute(s) that is common to both tables. The most common language associated with the relational model is the Structured Query Language (SQL), though it differs in some places.

Object model

In recent years, the object-oriented paradigm has been applied in areas such as engineering and spatial databases, telecommunications and in various scientific domains. The conglomeration of object oriented programming and database technology led to this new kind of database. These databases attempt to bring the database world and the application-programming world closer together, in particular by ensuring that the database uses the same type system as the application program. This aims to avoid the overhead (sometimes referred to as the *impedance mismatch*) of converting information between its representation in the database (for example as rows in tables) and its representation in the application program (typically as objects). At the same time, object databases attempt to introduce key ideas of object programming, such as encapsulation and polymorphism, into the world of databases.

A variety of these ways have been tried for storing objects in a database. Some products have approached the problem from the application-programming side, by making the objects manipulated by the program persistent. This also typically requires the addition of some kind of query language, since conventional programming languages do not provide language-level functionality for finding objects based on their information content. Others have attacked the problem from the database end, by defining an object-oriented data model for the database, and defining a database programming language that allows full programming capabilities as well as traditional query facilities.

Other database models

Products offering a more general data model than the relational model are sometimes classified as post-relational.[7] Alternate terms include "hybrid database", "Object-enhanced RDBMS" and others. The data model in such products incorporates relations but is not constrained by E.F. Codd's Information Principle, which requires that

all information in the database must be cast explicitly in terms of values in relations and in no other way[8]

Some of these extensions to the relational model integrate concepts from technologies that pre-date the relational model. For example, they allow representation of a directed graph with trees on the nodes. The German company *sones* implements this concept in its GraphDB.

Some post-relational products extend relational systems with non-relational features. Others arrived in much the same place by adding relational features to pre-relational systems. Paradoxically, this allows products that are historically pre-relational, such as PICK and MUMPS, to make a plausible claim to be post-relational.

The resource space model (RSM) is a non-relational data model based on multi-dimensional classification.[9]

Database languages

Database languages are dedicated programming languages, tailored and utilized to

- define a database (i.e., its specific data types and the relationships among them),
- manipulate its content (e.g., insert new data occurrences, and update or delete existing ones), and
- query it (i.e., request information: compute and retrieve any information based on its data).

Database languages are data-model-specific, i.e., each language assumes and is based on a certain structure of the data (which typically differs among different data models). They typically have commands to instruct execution of the desired operations in the database. Each such command is equivalent to a complex expression (program) in a regular programming language, and thus programming in dedicated (database) languages simplifies the task of handling databases considerably. An expressions in a database language is automatically transformed (by a compiler or interpreter, as regular programming languages) to a proper computer program that runs while accessing the database and providing the needed results. The following are notable examples:

SQL for the Relational model

A major Relational model language supported by all the relational DBMSs and a standard.

SQL was one of the first commercial languages for the relational model. Despite not adhering to the relational model as described by Codd, it has become the most widely used database language.[10] [11] Though often described as, and to a great extent is a declarative language, SQL also includes procedural elements. SQL became a standard of the American National Standards Institute (ANSI) in 1986, and of the International Organization for Standards (ISO) in 1987. Since then the standard has been enhanced several times with added features. However, issues of SQL code portability between major RDBMS products still exist due to lack of full compliance with, or different interpretations of the standard. Among the reasons mentioned are the large size, and incomplete specification of the standard, as well as vendor lock-in.

OQL for the Object model

An Object model language standard (by the Object Data Management Group) that has influenced the design of some of the newer query languages like JDOQL and EJB QL, though they cannot be considered as different flavors of OQL.

XQuery for the XML model

XQuery is an XML based database language (also named XQL).

Database architecture

Database architecture (to be distinguished from DBMS architecture; see below) may be viewed, to some extent, as an extension of Data modeling. It is used to conveniently answer requirements of different end-users from a same database, as well as for other benefits. For example, a financial department of a company needs the payment details of all employees as part of the company's expenses, but not other many details about employees, that are the interest of the human resources department. Thus different departments need different *views* of the company's database, that both include the employees' payments, possibly in a different level of detail (and presented in different visual forms). To meet such requirement effectively database architecture consists of three levels: *external*, *conceptual* and *internal*. Clearly separating the three levels was a major feature of the relational database model implementations that dominate 21st century databases.[12]

- The **external level** defines how each end-user type understands the organization of its respective relevant data in the database, i.e., the different needed end-user views. A single database can have any number of views at the external level.

- The **conceptual level** unifies the various external views into a coherent whole, global view.[12] It provides the common-denominator of all the external views. It comprises all the end-user needed generic data, i.e., all the data from which any view may be derived/computed. It is provided in the simplest possible way of such generic data, and comprises the back-bone of the database. It is out of the scope of the various database end-users, and serves database application developers and defined by database administrators that build the database.
- The **Internal level** (or *Physical level*) is as a matter of fact part of the database implementation inside a DBMS (see Implementation section below). It is concerned with cost, performance, scalability and other operational matters. It deals with storage layout of the conceptual level, provides supporting storage-structures like indexes, to enhance performance, and occasionally stores data of individual views (materialized views), computed from generic data, if performance justification exists for such redundancy. It balances all the external views' performance requirements, possibly conflicting, in attempt to optimize the overall database usage by all its end-uses according to the database goals and priorities.

All the three levels are maintained and updated according to changing needs by database administrators who often also participate in the database design.

The above three-level database architecture also relates to and being motivated by the concept of *data independence* which has been described for long time as a desired database property and was one of the major initial driving forces of the Relational model. In the context of the above architecture it means that changes made at a certain level do not affect definitions and software developed with higher level interfaces, and are being incorporated at the higher level automatically. For example, changes in the internal level do not affect application programs written using conceptual level interfaces, which saves substantial change work that would be needed otherwise.

In summary, the conceptual is a level of indirection between internal and external. On one hand it provides a common view of the database, independent of different external view structures, and on the other hand it is uncomplicated by details of how the data is stored or managed (internal level). In principle every level, and even every external view, can be presented by a different data model. In practice usually a given DBMS uses the same data model for both the external and the conceptual levels (e.g., relational model). The internal level, which is hidden inside the DBMS and depends on its implementation (see Implementation section below), requires a different level of detail and uses its own data structure types, typically different in nature from the structures of the external and conceptual levels which are exposed to DBMS users (e.g., the data models above): While the external and conceptual levels are focused on and serve DBMS users, the concern of the internal level is effective implementation details.

Database security

Database security deals with all various aspects of protecting the database content, its owners, and its users. It ranges from protection from intentional unauthorized database uses to unintentional database accesses by unauthorized entities (e.g., a person or a computer program).

The following are major areas of database security (among many others).

Access control

Database access control deals with controlling who (a person or a certain computer program) is allowed to access what information in the database. The information may comprise specific database objects (e.g., record types, specific records, data structures), certain computations over certain objects (e.g., query types, or specific queries), or utilizing specific access paths to the former (e.g., using specific indexes or other data structures to access information).

Database access controls are set by special authorized (by the database owner) personnel that uses dedicated protected security DBMS interfaces.

Data security

The definition of data security varies and may overlap with other database security aspects. Broadly it deals with protecting specific chunks of data, both physically (i.e., from corruption, or destruction, or removal; e.g., see Physical security), or the interpretation of them, or parts of them to meaningful information (e.g., by looking at the strings of bits that they comprise, concluding specific valid credit-card numbers; e.g., see Data encryption).

Database audit

Database audit primarily involves monitoring that no security breach, in all aspects, has happened. If security breach is discovered then all possible corrective actions are taken.

Database design

Database design is done before building it to meet needs of end-users within a given application/information-system that the database is intended to support. The database design defines the needed data and data structures that such a database comprises. A design is typically carried out according to the common three architectural levels of a database (see Database architecture above). First, the conceptual level is designed, which defines the over-all picture/view of the database, and reflects all the real-world elements (entities) the database intends to model, as well as the relationships among them. On top of it the external level, various views of the database, are designed according to (possibly completely different) needs of specific end-user types. More external views can be added later. External views requirements may modify the design of the conceptual level (i.e., add/remove entities and relationships), but usually a well designed conceptual level for an application well supports most of the needed external views. The conceptual view also determines the internal level (which primarily deals with data layout in storage) to a great extent. External views requirement may add supporting storage structures, like materialized views and indexes, for enhanced performance. Typically the internal layer is optimized for top performance, in an average way that takes into account performance requirements (possibly conflicting) of different external views according to their relative importance. While the conceptual and external levels design can usually be done independently of any DBMS (DBMS-independent design software packages exist, possibly with interfaces to some specific popular DBMSs), the internal level design highly relies on the capabilities and internal data structure of the specific DBMS utilized (see the Implementation section below).

A common way to carry out conceptual level design is to use the Entity-relationship model (ERM) (both the basic one, and with possible enhancement that it has gone over), since it provides a straightforward, intuitive perception of an application's elements and semantics. An alternative approach, which preceded the ERM, is using the Relational model and dependencies (mathematical relationships) among data to normalize the database, i.e., to define the ("optimal") relations (data record or tupple types) in the database. Though a large body of research exists for this method it is more complex, less intuitive, and not more effective than the ERM method. Thus normalization is less utilized in practice than the ERM method.

The ERM may be less subtle than normalization in several aspects, but it captures the main needed dependencies which are induced by keys/identifiers of entities and relationships. Also the ERM inherently includes the important inclusion dependencies (i.e., an entity instance that does not exist (has not been explicitly inserted) cannot appear in a relationship with other entities) which usually have been ignored in normalization.[13] In addition the ERM allows entity type generalization (the Is-a relationship) and implied property (attribute) inheritance (similarly to the that found in the Object model).

Another aspect of database design is its security. It involves both defining access control to database objects (e.g., Entities, Views) as well as defining security levels and methods for the data itself (See Database security above).

Entities and relationships

The most common database design methods are based on the Entity relationship model (ERM, or ER model). This model views the world in a simplistic but very powerful way: It consists of "Entities" and the "Relationships" among them. Accordingly a database consists of *entity* and *relationship* types, each with defined *attributes* (field types) that model concrete entities and relationships. Modeling a database in this way typically yields an effective one with desired properties (as in some *normal forms*; see normalization below). Such models can be translated to any other data model required by any specific DBMS for building an effective database.

Database normalization

In the design of a relational database, the process of organizing database relations to minimize redundancy is called *normalization*. The goal is to produce well-structured relations so that additions, deletions, and modifications of a field can be made in just one relation (table) without worrying about appearance and update of the same field in other relations. The process is algorithmic and based on dependencies (mathematical relations) that exist among relations' field types. The process result is bringing the database relations into a certain "normal form". Several normal forms exist with different properties.

Database building, maintaining, and tuning

After designing a database for an application arrives the stage of building the database. Typically an appropriate general-purpose DBMS can be selected to be utilized for this purpose. A DBMS provides the needed user interfaces to be utilized by database administrators to define the needed application's data structures within the DBMS's respective data model. Other user interfaces are used to select needed DBMS parameters (like security related, storage allocation parameters, etc.).

When the database is ready (all its data structures and other needed components are defined) it is typically populated with initial application's data (database initialization, which is typically a distinct project; in many cases using specialized DBMS interfaces that support bulk insertion) before making it operational. In some cases the database becomes operational while empty from application's data, and data are accumulated along its operation.

After completing building the database and making it operational arrives the database maintenance stage: Various database parameters may need changes and tuning for better performance, application's data structures may be changed or added, new related application programs may be written to add to the application's functionality, etc.

Miscellaneous areas

Database migration between DBMSs

  See also *Database migration* in *Data migration*

A database built with one DBMS is not portable to another DBMS (i.e., the other DBMS cannot run it). However, in some situations it is desirable to move, migrate a database from one DBMS to another. The reasons are primarily economical (different DBMSs may have different total costs of ownership-TCO), functional, and operational (different DBMSs may have different capabilities). The migration involves the database's transformation from one DBMS type to another. The transformation should maintain (if possible) the database related application (i.e., all related application programs) intact. Thus, the database's conceptual and external architectural levels should be maintained in the transformation. It may be desired that also some aspects of the architecture internal level are maintained. A complex or large database migration may be a complicated and costly (one-time) project by itself, which should be factored into the decision to migrate. This in spite of the fact that tools may exist to help migration between specific DBMS. Typically a DBMS vendor provides tools to help importing databases from other popular DBMSs.

Implementation: Database management systems

or **How database usage requirements are met** A *database management system* (DBMS) is a system that allows to build and maintain databases, as well as to utilize their data and retrieve information from it. A DBMS defines the database type that it supports, as well as its functionality and operational capabilities. A DBMS provides the internal processes for external applications built on them. The end-users of some such specific application are usually exposed only to that application and do not directly interact with the DBMS. Thus end-users enjoy the effects of the underlying DBMS, but its internals are completely invisible to end-users. Database designers and database administrators interact with the DBMS through dedicated interfaces to build and maintain the applications' databases, and thus need some more knowledge and understanding about how DBMSs operate and the DBMSs' external interfaces and tuning parameters.

A DBMS consists of software that operates databases, providing storage, access, security, backup and other facilities to meet needed requirements. DBMSs can be categorized according to the database model(s) that they support, such as relational or XML, the type(s) of computer they support, such as a server cluster or a mobile phone, the query language(s) that access the database, such as SQL or XQuery, performance trade-offs, such as maximum scale or maximum speed or others. Some DBMSs cover more than one entry in these categories, e.g., supporting multiple query languages. Database software typically support the Open Database Connectivity (ODBC) standard which allows the database to integrate (to some extent) with other databases.

The development of a mature general-purpose DBMS typically takes several years and many man-years. Developers of DBMS typically update their product to follow and take advantage of progress in computer and storage technologies. Several DBMS products like Oracle and IBM DB2 have been in on-going development since the 1970s-1980s. Since DBMSs comprise a significant economical market, computer and storage vendors often take into account DBMS requirements in their own development plans.

DBMS architecture: major DBMS components

DBMS architecture specifies its components (including descriptions of their functions) and their interfaces. DBMS architecture is distinct from database architecture. The following are major DBMS components:

- **DBMS external interfaces** - They are the means to communicate with the DBMS (both ways, to and from the DBMS) to perform all the operations needed for the DBMS. These can be operations on a database, or operations to operate and manage the DBMS. For example:

  - Direct database operations: defining data types, assigning security levels, updating data, querying the database, etc.

  - Operations related to DBMS operation and management: backup and restore, database recovery, security monitoring, database storage allocation and database layout configuration monitoring, performance monitoring and tuning, etc.

  An external interface can be either a *user interface* (e.g., typically for a database administrator), or an *application programming interface* (API) used for communication between an application program and the DBMS.

- **Database language engines** (or **processors**) - Most operations upon databases are performed through expression in Database languages (see above). Languages exist for data definition, data manipulation and queries (e.g., SQL), as well as for specifying various aspects of security, and more. Language expressions are fed into a DBMS through proper interfaces. A language engine processes the language expressions (by a compiler or language interpreter) to extract the intended database operations from the expression in a way that they can be executed by the DBMS.

- **Query optimizer** - Performs query optimization on every query to choose for it the most efficient *query plan* (a partial order (tree) of operations) to be executed to compute the query result.

- **Database engine** - Performs the received database operations on the database objects, typically at their higher-level representation.
- **Storage engine** - translates the operations to low-level operations on the storage bits. In some references the Storage engine is viewed as part of the Database engine.
- **Transaction engine** - for correctness and reliability purposes most DBMS internal operations are performed encapsulated in transactions (see below). Transactions can also be specified externally to the DBMS to encapsulate a group of operations. The transaction engine tracks all the transactions and manages their execution according to the transaction rules (e.g., proper concurrency control, and proper *commit* or *abort* for each).
- **DBMS management and operation component** - Comprises many components that deal with all the DBMS management and operational aspects like performance monitoring and tuning, backup and restore, recovery from failure, security management and monitoring, database storage allocation and database storage layout monitoring, etc.

Database storage

Database storage is the container of the physical materialization of a database. It comprises the *Internal* (physical) *level* in the database architecture. It also contains all the information needed (e.g., metadata, "data about the data", and internal data structures) to reconstruct the *Conceptual level* and *External level* from the Internal level when needed. It is not part of the DBMS but rather manipulated by the DBMS (by its Storage engine; see above) to manage the database that resides in it. Though typically accessed by a DBMS through the underlying Operating system (and often utilizing the operating systems' File systems as intermediates for storage layout), storage properties and configuration setting are extremely important for the efficient operation of the DBMS, and thus are closely maintained by database administrators. A DBMS, while in operation, always has its database residing in several types of storage (e.g., memory and external storage). The database data and the additional needed information, possibly in very large amounts, are coded into bits. Data typically reside in the storage in structures that look completely different from the way the data look in the conceptual and external levels, but in ways that attempt to optimize (the best possible) these levels' reconstruction when needed by users and programs, as well as for computing additional types of needed information from the data (e.g., when querying the database).

In principle the database storage can be viewed as a linear address space, where every bit of data has its unique address in this address space. Practically only a very small percentage of addresses is kept as initial reference points (which also requires storage), and most of the database data is accessed by indirection using displacement calculations (distance in bits from the reference points) and data structures which define access paths (using pointers) to all needed data in effective manner, optimized for the needed data access operations.

Data

Coding the data and Error-correcting codes

- Data is encoded by assigning a bit pattern to each language alphabet character, digit, other numerical patterns, and multimedia object. Many standards exist for encoding (e.g., ASCII, JPEG, MPEG-4).
- By adding bits to each encoded unit, the redundancy allows both to detect errors in coded data and to correct them based on mathematical algorithms. Errors occur regularly in low probabilities due to random bit value flipping, or "physical bit fatigue," loss of the physical bit in storage its ability to maintain distinguishable value (0 or 1), or due to errors in inter or intra-computer communication. A random bit flip (e.g., due to random radiation) is typically corrected upon detection. A bit, or a group of malfunctioning physical bits (not always the specific defective bit is known; group definition depends on specific storage device) is typically automatically fenced-out, taken out of use by the device, and replaced with another functioning equivalent group in the device, where the corrected bit values are restored (if possible). The Cyclic redundancy check (CRC) method is typically used in storage for error detection.

Data compression

Data compression methods allow in many cases to represent a string of bits by a shorter bit string ("compress") and reconstruct the original string ("decompress") when needed. This allows to utilize substantially less storage (tens of percents) for many types of data at the cost of more computation (compress and decompress when needed). Analysis of trade-off between storage cost saving and costs of related computations and possible delays in data availability is done before deciding whether to keep certain data in a database compressed or not.

Data compression is typically controlled through the DBMS's data definition interface, but in some cases may be a default and automatic.

Data encryption

For security reasons certain types of data (e.g., credit-card information) may be kept encrypted in storage to prevent the possibility of unauthorized information reconstruction from chunks of storage snapshots (taken either via unforeseen vulnerabilities in a DBMS, or more likely, by bypassing it).

Data encryption is typically controlled through the DBMS's data definition interface, but in some cases may be a default and automatic.

Data storage types

This collection of bits describes both the contained database data and its related metadata (i.e., data that describes the contained data and allows computer programs to manipulate the database data correctly). The size of a database can nowadays be tens of Terabytes, where a byte is eight bits. The physical materialization of a bit can employ various existing technologies, while new and improved technologies are constantly under development. Common examples are:

- *Magnetic medium* (e.g., in Magnetic disk) - Orientation of magnetic field in magnetic regions on a surface of material (two orientation directions, for 0 and 1).
- *Dynamic random-access memory* (DRAM) - State of a miniature electronic circuit consisting of few transistors (among millions nowadays) in an integrated circuit (two states for 0 and 1).

These two examples are respectively for two major storage types:

- *Nonvolatile storage* can maintain its bit states (0s and 1s) without electrical power supply, or when power supply is interrupted;
- *Volatile storage* loses its bit values when power supply is interrupted (i.e., its content is erased).

Sophisticated storage units, which can, in fact, be effective dedicated parallel computers that support a large amount of nonvolatile storage, typically must include also components with volatile storage. Some such units employ batteries that can provide power for several hours in case of external power interruption (e.g., see the EMC Symmetrix) and thus maintain the content of the volatile storage parts intact. Just before such a device's batteries lose their power the device typically automatically backs-up its volatile content portion (into nonvolatile) and shuts off to protect its data.

Databases are usually too expensive (in terms of importance and needed investment in resources, e.g., time, money, to build them) to be lost by a power interruption. Thus at any point in time most of their content resides in nonvolatile storage. Even if for operational reason very large portions of them reside in volatile storage (e.g., tens of Gigabytes in volatile memory, for in-memory databases), most of this is backed-up in nonvolatile storage. A relatively small portion of this, which temporarily may not have nonvolatile backup, can be reconstructed by proper automatic database recovery procedures after volatile storage content loss.

More examples of storage types:

- Volatile storage can be found in processors, computer memory (e.g., DRAM), etc.

- Non-volatile storage types include ROM, EPROM, Hard disk drives, Flash memory and drives, Storage arrays, etc.

Storage metrics

Databases always use several types of storage when operational (and implied several when idle). Different types may significantly differ in their properties, and the optimal mix of storage types is determined by the types and quantities of operations that each storage type needs to perform, as well as considerations like physical space and energy consumption and dissipation (which may become critical for a large database). Storage types can be categorized by the following attributes:

- Volatile/Nonvolatile.
- Cost of the medium (e.g., per Megabyte), Cost to operate (cost of energy consumed per unit time).
- Access speed (e.g., bytes per second).
- Granularity — from fine to coarse (e.g., size in bytes of access operation).
- Reliability (the probability of spontaneous bit value change under various conditions).
- Maximal possible number of writes (of any specific bit or specific group of bits; could be constrained by the technology used (e.g., "write once" or "write twice"), or due to "physical bit fatigue," loss of ability to distinguish between the 0, 1 states due to many state changes (e.g., in Flash memory)).
- Power needed to operate (Energy per time; energy per byte accessed), Energy efficiency, Heat to dissipate.
- Packaging density (e.g., realistic number of bytes per volume unit)

Protecting storage device content: Device mirroring (replication) and RAID

See also Disk storage replication

While a group of bits malfunction may be resolved by error detection and correction mechanisms (see above), storage device malfunction requires different solutions. The following solutions are commonly used and valid for most storage devices:

- **Device mirroring (replication)** - A common solution to the problem is constantly maintaining an identical copy of device content on another device (typically of a same type). The downside is that this doubles the storage, and both devices (copies) need to be updated simultaneously with some overhead and possibly some delays. The upside is possible concurrent read of a same data group by two independent processes, which increases performance. When one of the replicated devices is detected to be defective, the other copy is still operational, and is being utilized to generate a new copy on another device (usually available operational in a pool of stand-by devices for this purpose).
- **Redundant array of independent disks (RAID)** - This method generalizes the device mirroring above by allowing one device in a group of N devices to fail and be replaced with content restored (Device mirroring is RAID with N=2). RAID groups of N=5 or N=6 are common. N>2 saves storage, when comparing with N=2, at the cost of more processing during both regular operation (with often reduced performance) and defective device replacement.

Device mirroring and typical RAID are designed to handle a single device failure in the RAID group of devices. However, if a second failure occurs before the RAID group is completely repaired from the first failure, then data can be lost. The probability of a single failure is typically small. Thus the probability of two failures in a same RAID group in time proximity is much smaller (approximately the probability squared, i.e., multiplied by itself). If a database cannot tolerate even such smaller probability of data loss, then the RAID group itself is replicated (mirrored). In many cases such mirroring is done geographically remotely, in a different storage array, to handle also recovery from disasters (see disaster recovery above).

Database storage layout

Database bits are laid-out in storage in data-structures and grouping that can take advantage of both known effective algorithms to retrieve and manipulate them and the storage own properties. Typically the storage itself is design to meet requirements of various areas that extensively utilize storage, including databases. A DBMS in operation always simultaneously utilizes several storage types (e.g., memory, and external storage), with respective layout methods.

Database storage hierarchy

A database, while in operation, resides simultaneously in several types of storage. By the nature of contemporary computers most of the database part inside a computer that hosts the DBMS resides (partially replicated) in volatile storage. Data (pieces of the database) that are being processed/manipulated reside inside a processor, possibly in processor's caches. These data are being read from/written to memory, typically through a computer bus (so far typically volatile storage components). Computer memory is communicating data (transferred to/from) external storage, typically through standard storage interfaces or networks (e.g., fibre channel, iSCSI). A storage array, a common external storage unit, typically has storage hierarchy of it own, from a fast cache, typically consisting of (volatile and fast) DRAM, which is connected (again via standard interfaces) to drives, possibly with different speeds, like flash drives and magnetic disk drives (non-volatile). The drives may be connected to magnetic tapes, on which typically the least active parts of a large database may reside, or database backup generations.

Typically a correlation exists currently between storage speed and price, while the faster storage is typically volatile.

Data structures

A data structure is an abstract construct that embeds data in a well defined manner. An efficient data structure allows to manipulate the data in efficient ways. The data manipulation may include data insertion, deletion, updating and retrieval in various modes. A certain data structure type may be very effective in certain operations, and very ineffective in others. A data structure type is selected upon DBMS development to best meet the operations needed for the types of data it contains. Type of data structure selected for a certain task typically also takes into consideration the type of storage it resides in (e.g., speed of access, minimal size of storage chunk accessed, etc.). In some DBMSs database administrators have the flexibility to select among options of data structures to contain user data for performance reasons. Sometimes the data structures have selectable parameters to tune the database performance.

Databases may store data in many data structure types.[14] Common examples are the following:

- ordered/unordered flat files
- hash tables
- B+ trees
- ISAM
- heaps

Application data and DBMS data

A typical DBMS cannot store the data of the application it serves alone. In order to handle the application data the DBMS need to store this data in data structures that comprise specific data by themselves. In addition the DBMS needs its own data structures and many types of bookkeeping data like indexes and logs. The DBMS data is an integral part of the database and may comprise a substantial portion of it.

Database indexing

Indexing is a technique for improving database performance. The many types of indexes share the common property that they reduce the need to examine every entry when running a query. In large databases, this can reduce query time/cost by orders of magnitude. The simplest form of index is a sorted list of values that can be searched using a binary search with an adjacent reference to the location of the entry, analogous to the index in the back of a book. The same data can have multiple indexes (an employee database could be indexed by last name and hire date.)

Indexes affect performance, but not results. Database designers can add or remove indexes without changing application logic, reducing maintenance costs as the database grows and database usage evolves.

Given a particular query, the DBMS' query optimizer is responsible for devising the most efficient strategy for finding matching data.

Indexes can speed up data access, but they consume space in the database, and must be updated each time the data is altered. Indexes therefore can speed data access but slow data maintenance. These two properties determine whether a given index is worth the cost.

Database data clustering

In many cases substantial performance improvement is gained if different types of database objects that are usually utilized together are laid in storage in proximity, being *clustered*. This usually allows to retrieve needed related objects from storage in minimum number of input operations (each sometimes substantially time consuming). Even for in-memory databases clustering provides performance advantage due to common utilization of large caches for input-output operations in memory, with similar resulting behavior.

For example it may be beneficial to cluster a record of an *item* in stock with all its respective *order* records. The decision of whether to cluster certain objects or not depends on the objects' utilization statistics, object sizes, caches sizes, storage types, etc. In a relational database clustering the two respective relations "Items" and "Orders" results in saving the expensive execution of a Join operation between the two relations whenever such a join is needed in a query (the join result is already ready in storage by the clustering, available to be utilized).

Database materialized views

Often storage redundancy is employed to increase performance. A common example is storing *materialized views*, which are frequently-needed *External views*. Storing such external views saves expensive computing of them each time they are needed.

Database and database object replication

See also *Replication* below

Occasionally a database employs storage redundancy by database objects replication (with one or more copies) to increase data availability (both to improve performance of simultaneous multiple end-user accesses to a same database object, and to provide resiliency in a case of partial failure of a distributed database). Updates of a replicated object need to be synchronized across the object copies. In many cases the entire database is replicated.

Database transactions

As with every software system, a DBMS that operates in a faulty computing environment is prone to failures of many kinds. A failure can corrupt the respective database unless special measures are taken to prevent this. A DBMS achieves certain levels of fault tolerance by encapsulating operations within transactions. The concept of a *database transaction* (or *atomic transaction*) has evolved in order to enable both a well understood database system behavior in a faulty environment where crashes can happen any time, and *recovery* from a crash to a well understood database state. A database transaction is a unit of work, typically encapsulating a number of operations over a database (e.g., reading a database object, writing, acquiring lock, etc.), an abstraction supported in database and also other systems. Each transaction has well defined boundaries in terms of which program/code executions are included in that transaction (determined by the transaction's programmer via special transaction commands).

ACID rules

Every database transaction obeys the following rules:

- **Atomicity** - Either the effects of all or none of its operations remain ("all or nothing" semantics) when a transaction is completed (*committed* or *aborted* respectively). In other words, to the outside world a committed transaction appears (by its effects on the database) to be indivisible, atomic, and an aborted transaction does not leave effects on the database at all, as if never existed.
- **Consistency** - Every transaction must leave the database in a consistent (correct) state, i.e., maintain the predetermined integrity rules of the database (constraints upon and among the database's objects). A transaction must transform a database from one consistent state to another consistent state (however, it is the responsibility of the transaction's programmer to make sure that the transaction itself is correct, i.e., performs correctly what it intends to perform (from the application's point of view) while the predefined integrity rules are enforced by the DBMS). Thus since a database can be normally changed only by transactions, all the database's states are consistent. An aborted transaction does not change the database state it has started from, as if it never existed (atomicity above).
- **Isolation** - Transactions cannot interfere with each other (as an end result of their executions). Moreover, usually (depending on concurrency control method) the effects of an incomplete transaction are not even visible to another transaction. Providing isolation is the main goal of concurrency control.
- **Durability** - Effects of successful (committed) transactions must persist through crashes (typically by recording the transaction's effects and its commit event in a non-volatile memory).

Isolation, concurrency control, and locking

Isolation provides the ability for multiple users to operate on the database at the same time without corrupting the data.

- **Concurrency control** comprises the underlying mechanisms in a DBMS which handle isolation and guarantee related correctness. It is heavily utilized by the Database and Storage engines (see above) both to guarantee the correct execution of concurrent transactions, and (different mechanisms) the correctness of other DBMS processes. The transaction-related mechanisms typically constrain the database data access operations' timing (transaction schedules) to certain orders characterized as the Serializability and Recoverabiliry schedule properties. Constraining database access operation execution typically means reduced performance (rates of execution), and thus concurrency control mechanisms are typically designed to provide the best performance possible under the constraints. Often, when possible without harming correctness, the serializability property is compromised for better performance. However, recoverability cannot be compromised, since such typically results in a quick database integrity violation.
- **Locking** is the most common transaction concurrency control method in DBMSs, used to provide both serializability and recoverability for correctness. In order to access a database object a transaction first needs to acquire a lock for this object. Depending on the access operation type (e.g., reading or writing an object) and on

the lock type, acquiring the lock may be blocked and postponed, if another transaction is holding a lock for that object.

Query optimization

A query is a request for information from a database. It can be as simple as "finding the address of a person with SS# 123-123-1234," or more complex like "finding the average salary of all the employed married men in California between the ages 30 to 39, that earn less than their wives." Queries results are generated by accessing relevant database data and manipulating it in a way that yields the requested information. Since database structures are complex, in most cases, and especially for not-very-simple queries, the needed data for a query can be collected from a database by accessing it in different ways, through different data-structures, and in different orders. Each different way typically requires different processing time. Processing times of a same query may have large variance, from a fraction of a second to hours, depending on the way selected. The purpose of **query optimization**, which is an automated process, is to find the way to process a given query in minimum time. The large possible variance in time justifies performing query optimization, though finding the exact optimal way to execute a query, among all possibilities, is typically very complex, time consuming by itself, may be too costly, and often practically impossible. Thus query optimization typically tries to approximate the optimum by comparing several common-sense alternatives to provide in a reasonable time a "good enough" plan which typically does not deviate much from the best possible result.

DBMS support for the development and maintenance of a database and its application

A DBMS typically intends to provide convenient environment to develop and later maintain an application built around its respective database type. A DBMS either provides such tools, or allows integration with such external tools. Examples for tools relate to database design, application programming, application program maintenance, database performance analysis and monitoring, database configuration monitoring, DBMS hardware configuration (a DBMS and related database may span computers, networks, and storage units) and related database mapping (especially for a distributed DBMS), storage allocation and database layout monitoring, storage migration, etc.

See also

- Comparison of relational database management systems
- Comparison of database tools
- Data hierarchy
- Data store
- Database-centric architecture
- Database testing
- Glass database, a collection of glass compositions and related properties

References

[1] Jeffrey Ullman and Jennifer widom 1997: *First course in database systems*, Prentice-Hall Inc., Simon & Schuster, Page 1, ISBN 0-13-861337-0.

[2] C. W. Bachmann, *The Programmer as Navigator*

[3] Graves, Steve. "COTS Databases For Embedded Systems" (http://www.embedded-computing.com/articles/id/?2020), *Embedded Computing Design* magazine, January, 2007. Retrieved on August 13, 2008.

[4] "TeleCommunication Systems Signs up as a Reseller of TimesTen; Mobile Operators and Carriers Gain Real-Time Platform for Location-Based Services" (http://findarticles.com/p/articles/mi_m0EIN/is_2002_June_24/ai_87694370). *Business Wire*. 2002-06-24. .

[5] Argumentation in Artificial Intelligence by Iyad Rahwan, Guillermo R. Simari

[6] "OWL DL Semantics" (http://www.obitko.com/tutorials/ontologies-semantic-web/owl-dl-semantics.html). . Retrieved 10 December 2010.

[7] *Introducing databases* by Stephen Chu, in Conrick, M. (2006) *Health informatics: transforming healthcare with technology*, Thomson, ISBN 0-17-012731-1, p. 69.

[8] Date, C. J. (June 1, 1999). "When's an extension not an extension?" (http://intelligent-enterprise.informationweek.com/db_area/archives/1999/990106/online1.jhtml;jsessionid=Y2UNK1QFKXMBTQE1GHRSKH4ATMY32JVN). *Intelligent Enterprise* **2** (8). .

[9] Zhuge, H. (2008). *The Web Resource Space Model*. Web Information Systems Engineering and Internet Technologies Book Series. **4**. Springer. ISBN 978-0-387-72771-4.

[10] Chapple, Mike. "SQL Fundamentals" (http://databases.about.com/od/sql/a/sqlfundamentals.htm). *Databases*. About.com. . Retrieved 2009-01-28.

[11] "Structured Query Language (SQL)" (http://publib.boulder.ibm.com/infocenter/db2luw/v9/index.jsp?topic=com.ibm.db2.udb.admin.doc/doc/c0004100.htm). International Business Machines. October 27, 2006. . Retrieved 2007-06-10.

[12] Date 1990

[13] Johann A. Makowsky, Victor M. Markowitz and Nimrod Rotics, 1986: "Entity-relationship consistency for relational schemas" (http://www.springerlink.com/content/p67756164r127m18/) *Proceedings of the 1986 Conference on Database Theory* (ICDT '86), Lecture Notes in Computer Science, 1986, Volume 243/1986, pp. 306-322, Springer, doi:10.1007/3-540-17187-8_43

[14] Lightstone, Teorey & Nadeau 2007

Further reading

- Ling Liu and Tamer M. Özsu (Eds.) (2009). " Encyclopedia of Database Systems (http://www.springer.com/computer/database+management+&+information+retrieval/book/978-0-387-49616-0), 4100 p. 60 illus. ISBN 978-0-387-49616-0. Table of Content available at http://refworks.springer.com/mrw/index.php?id=1217

- Beynon-Davies, P. (2004). Database Systems. 3rd Edition. Palgrave, Houndmills, Basingstoke.

- Connolly, Thomas and Carolyn Begg. *Database Systems*. New York: Harlow, 2002.

- Date, C. J. (2003). *An Introduction to Database Systems, Fifth Edition*. Addison Wesley. ISBN 0-201-51381-1.

- Gray, J. and Reuter, A. *Transaction Processing: Concepts and Techniques*, 1st edition, Morgan Kaufmann Publishers, 1992.

- Kroenke, David M. and David J. Auer. *Database Concepts*. 3rd ed. New York: Prentice, 2007.

- Lightstone, S.; Teorey, T.; Nadeau, T. (2007). *Physical Database Design: the database professional's guide to exploiting indexes, views, storage, and more*. Morgan Kaufmann Press. ISBN 0-12-369389-6.

- Teorey, T.; Lightstone, S. and Nadeau, T. *Database Modeling & Design: Logical Design*, 4th edition, Morgan Kaufmann Press, 2005. ISBN 0-12-685352-5

External links

- Database (http://www.dmoz.org/Computers/Data_Formats/Database/) at the Open Directory Project

Computer_data_storage

Computer data storage, often called **storage** or **memory**, refers to computer components and recording media that retain digital data. Data storage is a core function and fundamental component of computers.

In contemporary usage, 'memory' usually refers to semiconductor storage read-write random-access memory, typically DRAM (Dynamic-RAM). *Memory* can refer to other forms of fast but temporary storage. *Storage* refers to storage devices and their media not directly accessible by the CPU, (secondary or tertiary storage), typically hard disk drives, optical disc drives, and other devices slower than RAM but are non-volatile (retaining contents when powered down).[1] Historically, *memory* has been called *core, main memory, real storage* or *internal memory* while storage devices have been referred to as *secondary storage, external memory* or *auxiliary/peripheral storage*.

1 GB of SDRAM mounted in a personal computer. An example of *primary* storage.

The distinctions are fundamental to the architecture of computers. The distinctions also reflect an important and significant technical difference between memory and mass storage devices, which has been blurred by the historical usage of the term *storage*. Nevertheless, this article uses the traditional nomenclature.

40 GB PATA hard disk drive (HDD); when connected to a computer it serves as *secondary* storage.

Many different forms of storage, based on various natural phenomena, have been invented. So far, no practical universal storage medium exists, and all forms of storage have some drawbacks. Therefore a computer system usually contains several kinds of storage, each with an individual purpose.

A modern digital computer represents data using the binary numeral system. Text, numbers, pictures, audio, and nearly any other form of information can be converted into a string of bits, or binary digits, each of which has a value of 1 or 0. The most common unit of storage is the byte, equal to 8 bits. A piece of information can be handled by any computer or device whose storage space is large enough to accommodate *the binary representation of the piece of information*, or simply data. For example, the complete works of Shakespeare, about 1250 pages in print, can be stored in about five megabytes (forty million bits) with one byte per character.

160 GB SDLT tape cartridge, an example of *off-line* storage. When used within a robotic tape library, it is classified as *tertiary* storage instead.

The defining component of a computer is the central processing unit (CPU, or simply processor), because it operates on data, performs computations, and controls other components. In the most commonly used computer architecture, the CPU consists of two main parts: Control Unit and Arithmetic Logic Unit (ALU). The former controls the flow of data between the CPU and memory; the later performs arithmetic and logical operations on data.

Without a significant amount of memory, a computer would merely be able to perform fixed operations and immediately output the result. It would have to be reconfigured to change its behavior. This is acceptable for devices such as desk calculators, digital signal processors, and other specialised devices. Von Neumann machines differ in having a memory in which they store their operating instructions and data. Such computers are more versatile in that they do not need to have their hardware reconfigured for each new program, but can simply be reprogrammed with new in-memory instructions; they also tend to be simpler to design, in that a relatively simple processor may keep state between successive computations to build up complex procedural results. Most modern computers are von Neumann machines.

In practice, almost all computers use a variety of memory types, organized in a storage hierarchy around the CPU, as a trade-off between performance and cost. Generally, the lower a storage is in the hierarchy, the lesser its bandwidth and the greater its access latency is from the CPU. This traditional division of storage to primary, secondary, tertiary and off-line storage is also guided by cost per bit.

Hierarchy of storage

Primary storage

Direct links to this section: Primary storage, Main memory, Internal Memory.

Primary storage (or *main memory* or *internal memory*), often referred to simply as *memory*, is the only one directly accessible to the CPU. The CPU continuously reads instructions stored there and executes them as required. Any data actively operated on is also stored there in uniform manner.

Historically, early computers used delay lines, Williams tubes, or rotating magnetic drums as primary storage. By 1954, those unreliable methods were mostly replaced by magnetic core memory. Core memory remained dominant until the 1970s, when advances in integrated circuit technology allowed semiconductor memory to become economically competitive.

This led to modern random-access memory (RAM). It is small-sized, light, but quite expensive at the same time. (The particular types of RAM used for primary storage are also volatile, i.e. they lose the information when not powered).

As shown in the diagram, traditionally there are two more sub-layers of the primary storage, besides main large-capacity RAM:

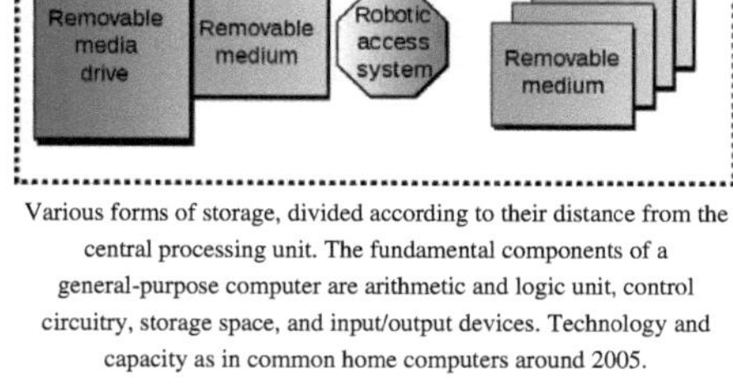

Various forms of storage, divided according to their distance from the central processing unit. The fundamental components of a general-purpose computer are arithmetic and logic unit, control circuitry, storage space, and input/output devices. Technology and capacity as in common home computers around 2005.

- Processor registers are located inside the processor. Each register typically holds a word of data (often 32 or 64 bits). CPU instructions instruct the arithmetic and logic unit to perform various calculations or other operations on this data (or with the help of it). Registers are the fastest of all forms of computer data storage.

- Processor cache is an intermediate stage between ultra-fast registers and much slower main memory. It's introduced solely to increase performance of the computer. Most actively used information in the main memory is just duplicated in the cache memory, which is faster, but of much lesser capacity. On the other hand, main memory is much slower, but has a much greater storage capacity than processor registers. Multi-level hierarchical cache setup is also commonly used—*primary cache* being smallest, fastest and located inside the processor; *secondary cache* being somewhat larger and slower.

Main memory is directly or indirectly connected to the central processing unit via a *memory bus*. It is actually two buses (not on the diagram): an address bus and a data bus. The CPU firstly sends a number through an address bus, a number called memory address, that indicates the desired location of data. Then it reads or writes the data itself using the data bus. Additionally, a memory management unit (MMU) is a small device between CPU and RAM recalculating the actual memory address, for example to provide an abstraction of virtual memory or other tasks.

As the RAM types used for primary storage are volatile (cleared at start up), a computer containing only such storage would not have a source to read instructions from, in order to start the computer. Hence, non-volatile primary storage containing a small startup program (BIOS) is used to bootstrap the computer, that is, to read a larger program from non-volatile *secondary* storage to RAM and start to execute it. A non-volatile technology used for this purpose is called ROM, for read-only memory (the terminology may be somewhat confusing as most ROM types are also capable of *random access*).

Many types of "ROM" are not literally *read only*, as updates are possible; however it is slow and memory must be erased in large portions before it can be re-written. Some embedded systems run programs directly from ROM (or similar), because such programs are rarely changed. Standard computers do not store non-rudimentary programs in ROM, rather use large capacities of secondary storage, which is non-volatile as well, and not as costly.

Recently, *primary storage* and *secondary storage* in some uses refer to what was historically called, respectively, *secondary storage* and *tertiary storage*.[2]

Secondary storage

Secondary storage (also known as external memory or auxiliary storage), differs from primary storage in that it is not directly accessible by the CPU. The computer usually uses its input/output channels to access secondary storage and transfers the desired data using intermediate area in primary storage. Secondary storage does not lose the data when the device is powered down—it is non-volatile. Per unit, it is typically also two orders of magnitude less expensive than primary storage. Consequently, modern computer systems typically have two orders of magnitude more secondary storage than primary storage and data are kept for a longer time there.

A hard disk drive with protective cover removed.

In modern computers, hard disk drives are usually used as secondary storage. The time taken to access a given byte of information stored on a hard disk is typically a few thousandths of a second, or milliseconds. By contrast, the time taken to access a given byte of information stored in random access memory is measured in billionths of a second, or nanoseconds. This illustrates the significant access-time difference which distinguishes solid-state memory from rotating magnetic storage devices: hard disks are typically about a million times slower than memory. Rotating optical storage devices, such as CD and DVD drives, have even longer access times. With disk drives, once the disk read/write head reaches the proper placement and the data of interest rotates under it, subsequent data on the track are very fast to access. As a result, in order to hide the initial seek time and rotational latency, data are transferred to and from disks in large contiguous blocks.

When data reside on disk, block access to hide latency offers a ray of hope in designing efficient external memory algorithms. Sequential or block access on disks is orders of magnitude faster than random access, and many sophisticated paradigms have been developed to design efficient algorithms based upon sequential and block access. Another way to reduce the I/O bottleneck is to use multiple disks in parallel in order to increase the bandwidth between primary and secondary memory.[3]

Some other examples of secondary storage technologies are: flash memory (e.g. USB flash drives or keys), floppy disks, magnetic tape, paper tape, punched cards, standalone RAM disks, and Iomega Zip drives.

The secondary storage is often formatted according to a file system format, which provides the abstraction necessary to organize data into files and directories, providing also additional information (called metadata) describing the owner of a certain file, the access time, the access permissions, and other information.

Most computer operating systems use the concept of virtual memory, allowing utilization of more primary storage capacity than is physically available in the system. As the primary memory fills up, the system moves the least-used chunks (*pages*) to secondary storage devices (to a swap file or page file), retrieving them later when they are needed. As more of these retrievals from slower secondary storage are necessary, the more the overall system performance is degraded.

Tertiary storage

Tertiary storage or *tertiary memory*,[4] provides a third level of storage. Typically it involves a robotic mechanism which will *mount* (insert) and *dismount* removable mass storage media into a storage device according to the system's demands; these data are often copied to secondary storage before use. It is primarily used for archiving rarely accessed information since it is much slower than secondary storage (e.g. 5–60 seconds vs. 1–10 milliseconds). This is primarily useful for extraordinarily large data stores, accessed without human operators. Typical examples include tape libraries and optical jukeboxes.

When a computer needs to read information from the tertiary storage, it will first consult a catalog database to determine which tape or disc contains the information. Next, the computer will instruct a robotic arm to fetch the medium and place it in a drive. When the computer has finished reading the information, the robotic arm will return the medium to its place in the library.

Large tape library. Tape cartridges placed on shelves in the front, robotic arm moving in the back. Visible height of the library is about 180 cm.

Off-line storage

Off-line storage is a computer data storage on a medium or a device that is not under the control of a processing unit.[5] The medium is recorded, usually in a secondary or tertiary storage device, and then physically removed or disconnected. It must be inserted or connected by a human operator before a computer can access it again. Unlike tertiary storage, it cannot be accessed without human interaction.

Off-line storage is used to transfer information, since the detached medium can be easily physically transported. Additionally, in case a disaster, for example a fire, destroys the original data, a medium in a remote location will probably be unaffected, enabling disaster recovery. Off-line storage increases general information security, since it is physically inaccessible from a computer, and data confidentiality or integrity cannot be affected by computer-based attack techniques. Also, if the information stored for archival purposes is rarely accessed, off-line storage is less expensive than tertiary storage.

In modern personal computers, most secondary and tertiary storage media are also used for off-line storage. Optical discs and flash memory devices are most popular, and to much lesser extent removable hard disk drives. In enterprise uses, magnetic tape is predominant. Older examples are floppy disks, Zip disks, or punched cards.

Characteristics of storage

Storage technologies at all levels of the storage hierarchy can be differentiated by evaluating certain core characteristics as well as measuring characteristics specific to a particular implementation. These core characteristics are volatility, mutability, accessibility, and addressibility. For any particular implementation of any storage technology, the characteristics worth measuring are capacity and performance.

Volatility

Non-volatile memory

> Will retain the stored information even if it is not constantly supplied with electric power. It is suitable for long-term storage of information.

Volatile memory

> Requires constant power to maintain the stored information. The fastest memory technologies of today are volatile ones (not a universal rule). Since primary storage is required to be very fast, it predominantly uses volatile memory.

A 1GB DDR RAM module (detail)

Dynamic random-access memory

> A form of volatile memory which also requires the stored information to be periodically re-read and re-written, or refreshed, otherwise it would vanish.

Static random-access memory

> A form of volatile memory similar to DRAM with the exception that it never needs to be refreshed as long as power is applied. (It loses its content if power is removed).

Mutability

Read/write storage or mutable storage

> Allows information to be overwritten at any time. A computer without some amount of read/write storage for primary storage purposes would be useless for many tasks. Modern computers typically use read/write storage also for secondary storage.

Read only storage

> Retains the information stored at the time of manufacture, and *write once storage* (Write Once Read Many) allows the information to be written only once at some point after manufacture. These are called *immutable storage*. Immutable storage is used for tertiary and off-line storage. Examples include CD-ROM and CD-R.

Slow write, fast read storage

> Read/write storage which allows information to be overwritten multiple times, but with the write operation being much slower than the read operation. Examples include CD-RW and flash memory.

Accessibility

Random access

Any location in storage can be accessed at any moment in approximately the same amount of time. Such characteristic is well suited for primary and secondary storage. Most semiconductor memories and disk drives provide random access.

Sequential access

The accessing of pieces of information will be in a serial order, one after the other; therefore the time to access a particular piece of information depends upon which piece of information was last accessed. Such characteristic is typical of off-line storage.

Addressability

Location-addressable

Each individually accessible unit of information in storage is selected with its numerical memory address. In modern computers, location-addressable storage usually limits to primary storage, accessed internally by computer programs, since location-addressability is very efficient, but burdensome for humans.

File addressable

Information is divided into *files* of variable length, and a particular file is selected with human-readable directory and file names. The underlying device is still location-addressable, but the operating system of a computer provides the file system abstraction to make the operation more understandable. In modern computers, secondary, tertiary and off-line storage use file systems.

Content-addressable

Each individually accessible unit of information is selected based on the basis of (part of) the contents stored there. Content-addressable storage can be implemented using software (computer program) or hardware (computer device), with hardware being faster but more expensive option. Hardware content addressable memory is often used in a computer's CPU cache.

CAS(content-addressable storage) addresses the thinking behind how are we to find and access the information that we currently have or will gather in the future.

Capacity

Raw capacity

The total amount of stored information that a storage device or medium can hold. It is expressed as a quantity of bits or bytes (e.g. 10.4 megabytes).

Memory storage density

The compactness of stored information. It is the storage capacity of a medium divided with a unit of length, area or volume (e.g. 1.2 megabytes per square inch).

Performance

Latency

The time it takes to access a particular location in storage. The relevant unit of measurement is typically nanosecond for primary storage, millisecond for secondary storage, and second for tertiary storage. It may make sense to separate read latency and write latency, and in case of sequential access storage, minimum, maximum and average latency.

Throughput

The rate at which information can be read from or written to the storage. In computer data storage, throughput is usually expressed in terms of megabytes per second or MB/s, though bit rate may also be used. As with latency, read rate and write rate may need to be differentiated. Also accessing media sequentially, as opposed to randomly, typically yields maximum throughput.

Energy use

- Storage devices that reduce fan usage, automatically shut-down during inactivity, and low power hard drives can reduce energy consumption 90 percent.[6]
- 2.5 inch hard disk drives often consume less power than larger ones.[7] [8] Low capacity solid-state drives have no moving parts and consume less power than hard disks.[9] [10] [11] Also, memory may use more power than hard disks.[11]

Fundamental storage technologies

As of 2011, the most commonly used data storage technologies are semiconductor, magnetic, and optical, while paper still sees some limited usage. *Media* is a common name for what actually holds the data in the storage device. Some other fundamental storage technologies have also been used in the past or are proposed for development.

Semiconductor

Semiconductor memory uses semiconductor-based integrated circuits to store information. A semiconductor memory chip may contain millions of tiny transistors or capacitors. Both *volatile* and *non-volatile* forms of semiconductor memory exist. In modern computers, primary storage almost exclusively consists of dynamic volatile semiconductor memory or dynamic random access memory. Since the turn of the century, a type of non-volatile semiconductor memory known as flash memory has steadily gained share as off-line storage for home computers. Non-volatile semiconductor memory is also used for secondary storage in various advanced electronic devices and specialized computers. As early as 2006, notebook and desktop computer manufacturers started using flash-based solid-state drives (SSDs) as default configuration options for the secondary storage either in addition to or instead of the more traditional HDD.[12] [13] [14] [15] [16]

Magnetic

Magnetic storage uses different patterns of magnetization on a magnetically coated surface to store information. Magnetic storage is *non-volatile*. The information is accessed using one or more read/write heads which may contain one or more recording transducers. A read/write head only covers a part of the surface so that the head or medium or both must be moved relative to another in order to access data. In modern computers, magnetic storage will take these forms:

- Magnetic disk
  - Floppy disk, used for off-line storage
  - Hard disk drive, used for secondary storage
- Magnetic tape, used for tertiary and off-line storage

In early computers, magnetic storage was also used as:

- Primary storage in a form of magnetic memory, or core memory, core rope memory, thin-film memory and/or twistor memory.
- Tertiary (e.g. NCR CRAM) or off line storage in the form of magnetic cards.
- Magnetic tape was then often used for secondary storage.

Optical

Optical storage, the typical optical disc, stores information in deformities on the surface of a circular disc and reads this information by illuminating the surface with a laser diode and observing the reflection. Optical disc storage is *non-volatile*. The deformities may be permanent (read only media), formed once (write once media) or reversible (recordable or read/write media). The following forms are currently in common use:[17]

- CD, CD-ROM, DVD, BD-ROM: Read only storage, used for mass distribution of digital information (music, video, computer programs)
- CD-R, DVD-R, DVD+R, BD-R: Write once storage, used for tertiary and off-line storage
- CD-RW, DVD-RW, DVD+RW, DVD-RAM, BD-RE: Slow write, fast read storage, used for tertiary and off-line storage
- Ultra Density Optical or UDO is similar in capacity to BD-R or BD-RE and is slow write, fast read storage used for tertiary and off-line storage.

Magneto-optical disc storage is optical disc storage where the magnetic state on a ferromagnetic surface stores information. The information is read optically and written by combining magnetic and optical methods. Magneto-optical disc storage is *non-volatile*, *sequential access*, slow write, fast read storage used for tertiary and off-line storage.

3D optical data storage has also been proposed.

Paper

Paper data storage, typically in the form of paper tape or punched cards, has long been used to store information for automatic processing, particularly before general-purpose computers existed. Information was recorded by punching holes into the paper or cardboard medium and was read mechanically (or later optically) to determine whether a particular location on the medium was solid or contained a hole. A few technologies allow people to make marks on paper that are easily read by machine—these are widely used for tabulating votes and grading standardized tests. Barcodes made it possible for any object that was to be sold or transported to have some computer readable information securely attached to it.

Uncommon

Vacuum tube memory

> A Williams tube used a cathode ray tube, and a Selectron tube used a large vacuum tube to store information. These primary storage devices were short-lived in the market, since Williams tube was unreliable and the Selectron tube was expensive.

Electro-acoustic memory

> Delay line memory used sound waves in a substance such as mercury to store information. Delay line memory was dynamic volatile, cycle sequential read/write storage, and was used for primary storage.

Optical tape

> is a medium for optical storage generally consisting of a long and narrow strip of plastic onto which patterns can be written and from which the patterns can be read back. It shares some technologies with cinema film stock and optical discs, but is compatible with neither. The motivation behind developing this technology was the possibility of far greater storage capacities than either magnetic tape or optical discs.

Phase-change memory

> uses different mechanical phases of Phase Change Material to store information in an X-Y addressable matrix, and reads the information by observing the varying electrical resistance of the material. Phase-change memory would be non-volatile, random access read/write storage, and might be used for primary, secondary and

off-line storage. Most rewritable and many write once optical disks already use phase change material to store information.

Holographic data storage

stores information optically inside crystals or photopolymers. Holographic storage can utilize the whole volume of the storage medium, unlike optical disc storage which is limited to a small number of surface layers. Holographic storage would be non-volatile, sequential access, and either write once or read/write storage. It might be used for secondary and off-line storage. See Holographic Versatile Disc (HVD).

Molecular memory

stores information in polymer that can store electric charge. Molecular memory might be especially suited for primary storage. The theoretical storage capacity of molecular memory is 10 terabits per square inch.[18]

Related technologies

Network connectivity

A secondary or tertiary storage may connect to a computer utilizing computer networks. This concept does not pertain to the primary storage, which is shared between multiple processors in a much lesser degree.

- Direct-attached storage (DAS) is a traditional mass storage, that does not use any network. This is still a most popular approach. This retronym was coined recently, together with NAS and SAN.
- Network-attached storage (NAS) is mass storage attached to a computer which another computer can access at file level over a local area network, a private wide area network, or in the case of online file storage, over the Internet. NAS is commonly associated with the NFS and CIFS/SMB protocols.
- Storage area network (SAN) is a specialized network, that provides other computers with storage capacity. The crucial difference between NAS and SAN is the former presents and manages file systems to client computers, whilst the latter provides access at block-addressing (raw) level, leaving it to attaching systems to manage data or file systems within the provided capacity. SAN is commonly associated with Fibre Channel networks.

Robotic storage

Large quantities of individual magnetic tapes, and optical or magneto-optical discs may be stored in robotic tertiary storage devices. In tape storage field they are known as tape libraries, and in optical storage field optical jukeboxes, or optical disk libraries per analogy. Smallest forms of either technology containing just one drive device are referred to as autoloaders or autochangers.

Robotic-access storage devices may have a number of slots, each holding individual media, and usually one or more picking robots that traverse the slots and load media to built-in drives. The arrangement of the slots and picking devices affects performance. Important characteristics of such storage are possible expansion options: adding slots, modules, drives, robots. Tape libraries may have from 10 to more than 100,000 slots, and provide terabytes or petabytes of near-line information. Optical jukeboxes are somewhat smaller solutions, up to 1,000 slots.

Robotic storage is used for backups, and for high-capacity archives in imaging, medical, and video industries. Hierarchical storage management is a most known archiving strategy of automatically *migrating* long-unused files from fast hard disk storage to libraries or jukeboxes. If the files are needed, they are *retrieved* back to disk.

See also

Primary storage topics

- Aperture (computer memory)
- Dynamic random access memory (DRAM)
- Memory latency
- Mass storage
- Memory cell (disambiguation)
- Memory management
  - Dynamic memory allocation
    - Memory leak
  - Virtual memory
- Memory protection
- Page address register
- Static random access memory (SRAM)
- Stable storage

Secondary, tertiary and off-line storage topics

- Data deduplication
- Data proliferation
- Data storage tag used for capturing research data
- File system
  - List of file formats
- Flash memory
- Information repository
- Removable media
- Solid-state drive
- Spindle
- Virtual tape library
- Wait state
- Write buffer
- Write protection

Data storage conferences

- Storage Networking World
- Storage World Conference

References

⊛ *This article incorporates public domain material from websites or documents of the General Services Administration.*

[1] *Storage* as defined in Microsoft Computing Dictionary, 4th Ed. (c)1999 or in The Authoritative Dictionary of IEEE Standard Terms, 7th Ed., (c) 2000.

[2] "Primary Storage or Storage Hardware" (shows usage of term "primary storage" meaning "hard disk storage") (http://searchstorage. techtarget.com/topics/0,295493,sid5_tax298620,00.html). Searchstorage.techtarget.com (2011-06-13). Retrieved on 2011-06-18.

[3] J. S. Vitter, *Algorithms and Data Structures for External Memory* (http://faculty.cse.tamu.edu/jsv/Papers/Vit.IO_book.pdf), Series on Foundations and Trends in Theoretical Computer Science, now Publishers, Hanover, MA, 2008, ISBN 978-1-60198-106-6.

[4]   A thesis on Tertiary storage (http://www.eecs.berkeley.edu/Pubs/TechRpts/1994/CSD-94-847.pdf). (PDF) . Retrieved on 2011-06-18.

[5]   National Communications System (1996). *Federal Standard 1037C — Telecommunications: Glossary of Telecommunication Terms* (http://www.its.bldrdoc.gov/fs-1037/fs-1037c.htm). General Services Administration. FS-1037C. . Retrieved 2007-10-08 See also article Federal Standard 1037C.

[6]   Energy Savings Calculator (http://www.springlightcfl.com/consumer/energy_savings_calculator.aspx) and Fabric website (http://www.simpletech.com/content/eco-friendly-redrive)

[7]   Mike Chin (8 March 2004). "IS the Silent PC Future 2.5-inches wide?" (http://www.silentpcreview.com/article145-page1.html). . Retrieved 2008-08-02.

[8]   Mike Chin (2002-09-18). "Recommended Hard Drives" (http://www.silentpcreview.com/article29-page2.html). . Retrieved 2008-08-02.

[9]   Super Talent's 2.5" IDE Flash hard drive — The Tech Report — Page 13 (http://techreport.com/articles.x/10334/13). The Tech Report. Retrieved on 2011-06-18.

[10]   Power Consumption — Tom's Hardware : Conventional Hard Drive Obsoletism? Samsung's 32 GB Flash Drive Previewed (http://www.tomshardware.com/reviews/conventional-hard-drive-obsoletism,1324-5.html). Tomshardware.com (2006-09-20). Retrieved on 2011-06-18.

[11]   Aleksey Meyev (2008-04-23). "SSD, i-RAM and Traditional Hard Disk Drives" (http://www.xbitlabs.com/articles/storage/display/ssd-iram.html). .

[12]   New Samsung Notebook Replaces Hard Drive With Flash (http://www.extremetech.com/article2/0,1558,1966644,00.asp). ExtremeTech (2006-05-23). Retrieved on 2011-06-18.

[13]   Welcome to TechNewsWorld (http://www.technewsworld.com/rsstory/60700.html?wlc=1308338527). Technewsworld.com. Retrieved on 2011-06-18.

[14]   Mac Pro — Storage and RAID options for your Mac Pro (http://www.apple.com/macpro/features/storage.html). Apple (2006-07-27). Retrieved on 2011-06-18.

[15]   MacBook Air — The best of iPad meets the best of Mac (http://www.apple.com/macbookair/design.html). Apple. Retrieved on 2011-06-18.

[16]   MacBook Air Replaces the Standard Notebook Hard Disk for Solid State Flash Storage (http://news.inventhelp.com/Articles/Computer/Inventions/apple-macbook-air-12512.aspx). News.inventhelp.com (2010-11-15). Retrieved on 2011-06-18.

[17]   The DVD FAQ (http://www.dvddemystified.com/dvdfaq.html) is a comprehensive reference of DVD technologies.

[18]   New Method Of Self-assembling Nanoscale Elements Could Transform Data Storage Industry (http://www.sciencedaily.com/releases/2009/02/090219141438.htm). Sciencedaily.com (2009-03-01). Retrieved on 2011-06-18.

Lookup

In computing, **lookup** usually refers to searching a data structure for an *item* that satisfies some specified *property*. (Note that in grammatical usage, *lookup* is the noun form describing the verb form *to look up*.) For example, variable lookup performed by a (scripting) language interpreter, virtual machine or other similar engine usually consists of performing certain actions to dynamically find correspondence between variable identifier and actual variable internal representation, usually involving symbol table lookup. Symbol table lookup can be performed either during run-time (interpreter or scripting engine), or during compile time (compiler). A hybrid scheme when lookup is performed both during translation phase and then later during runtime is also possible (e.g. bytecode compiler and virtual machine). In all of these cases, search *item* is a variable and the search *property* (or search criterion) is a variable name. Variable lookup is usually performed according to variable visibility rules that are specific to the (scripting) language in question.

Another example is DNS lookup. In DNS lookup, a DNS server is requested to find a host IP address given host domain name. Here the search criterion (*property*) is a domain name and the search result (*item*) is an IP address. A domain name may be associated with several IP addresses. Reverse DNS lookup performs the reverse task: given IP address, it attempts to resolve domain name associated with the specified IP address.

Spreadsheet software typically has functions such as LOOKUP, HLOOKUP, and VLOOKUP, to find either a value in a row or column that matches the argument, or in the case of **range lookup**, to find an interval in a set of adjacent intervals (given by their limits, specified in a row or column) which contains the argument. The result is the corresponding value in a specified parallel row or column.

Network_model

The **network model** is a database model conceived as a flexible way of representing objects and their relationships. Its distinguishing feature is that the schema, viewed as a graph in which object types are nodes and relationship types are arcs, is not restricted to being a hierarchy or lattice.

The network model's original inventor was Charles Bachman, and it was developed into a standard specification published in 1969 by the CODASYL Consortium.

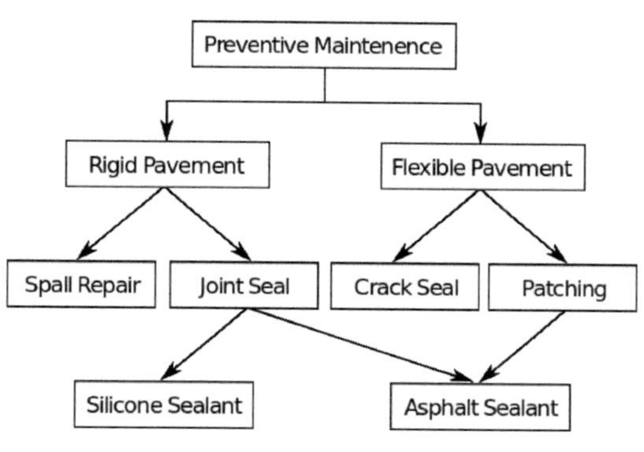

Example of a Network Model.

Overview

While the hierarchical database model structures data as a tree of records, with each record having one parent record and many children, the network model allows each record to have multiple parent and child records, forming a generalized graph structure. This property applies at two levels: the schema is a generalized graph of record types connected by relationship types (called "set types" in CODASYL), and the database itself is a generalized graph of record occurrences connected by relationships (CODASYL "sets"). Cycles are permitted at both levels.

The chief argument in favour of the network model, in comparison to the hierarchic model, was that it allowed a more natural modeling of relationships between entities. Although the model was widely implemented and used, it failed to become dominant for two main reasons. Firstly, IBM chose to stick to the hierarchical model with semi-network extensions in their established products such as IMS and DL/I. Secondly, it was eventually displaced by the relational model, which offered a higher-level, more declarative interface. Until the early 1980s the performance benefits of the low-level navigational interfaces offered by hierarchical and network databases were persuasive for many large-scale applications, but as hardware became faster, the extra productivity and flexibility of the relational model led to the gradual obsolescence of the network model in corporate enterprise usage.

Database systems

Some well-known database systems that use the network model include:

- Digital Equipment corporation DBMS-10
- Digital Equipment Corporation DBMS-20
- Digital Equipment Corporation VAX DBMS
- Honeywell IDS (Integrated Data Store)
- IDMS (Integrated Database Management System)
- RDM Embedded
- RDM Server
- TurboIMAGE
- Univac DMS-1100

History

In 1969, the Conference on Data Systems Languages (CODASYL) established the first specification of the network database model. This was followed by a second publication in 1971, which became the basis for most implementations. Subsequent work continued into the early 1980s, culminating in an ISO specification, but this had little influence on products.

See also

- CODASYL
- Navigational database
- Graph database

Further reading

- Charles W. Bachman, *The Programmer as Navigator*. ACM Turing Award lecture, Communications of the ACM, Volume 16, Issue 11, 1973, pp. 653-658, ISSN 0001-0782, doi:10.1145/355611.362534

External links

- CODASYL Systems Committee "Survey of Data Base Systems", 1968 [1] (edited and annotated in 2007 by Ken North)
- Network (CODASYL) Data Model [2]

References

[1] http://www.sqlsummit.com/PDF/DatabaseSurvey_CODASYL_1968.pdf
[2] http://coronet.iicm.edu/wbtmaster/allcoursescontent/netlib/ndm1.htm

Triplestore

A **triplestore** is a purpose-built database for the storage and retrieval of triples,[1] a triple being a data entity composed of subject-predicate-object, like "Bob is 35" or "Bob knows Fred".

Much like a relational database, one stores information in a triplestore and retrieves it via a query language. Unlike a relational database, a triplestore is optimized for the storage and retrieval of triples. In addition to queries, triples can usually be imported/exported using Resource Description Framework (RDF) and other formats.

Some triplestores can store billions of triples.[2] The performance of a particular triplestore can be measured with the Lehigh University Benchmark (LUBM),[3] or with real data from UniProt.

Implementation

Some triplestores have been built as database engines from scratch, while others have been built on top of existing commercial relational database engines (i.e. SQL-based).[4] Like the early development of online analytical processing (OLAP) databases, this intermediate approach allowed large and powerful database engines to be constructed for little programming effort in the initial phases of triplestore development. Long-term though it seems likely that native triplestores will have the advantage for performance. A difficulty with implementing triplestores over SQL is that although *triples* may thus be *stored*, implementing efficient querying of a graph-based RDF model (i.e. mapping from SPARQL) onto SQL queries is difficult.[5]

List of implementations

Name	Language	Homepage	Licence
3store	C	www.aktors.org/technologies/3store [6]	
4store	C	[www.4store.org www.4store.org]	GPL v3
5store	C	4store.org/trac/wiki/5store [7]	
AllegroGraph	Common Lisp	www.franz.com/agraph/allegrograph [8]	
ARC	PHP	[arc.semsol.org arc.semsol.org]	
Ariadne Genomics	Java	[www.ariadnegenomics.com www.ariadnegenomics.com]	
Bigdata	Java	[www.bigdata.com www.bigdata.com]	
BigOWLIM	Java	www.ontotext.com/owlim [9]	
BrightstarDB	C#	[brightstardb.com brightstardb.com]	
Dydra	Common Lisp, C	[www.dydra.com www.dydra.com]	
Apache Jena	Java	incubator.apache.org/jena/ [10]	
Mulgara	Java	[www.mulgara.org www.mulgara.org]	
OpenAnzo	Java	[www.openanzo.org www.openanzo.org]	
OntoBroker	Java	www.ontoprise.de/en/home/products/ontobroker [11]	
Oracle	Java, PL/SQL, SQL	www.oracle.com/technetwork/database/options/semantic-tech/whatsnew [12]	
Meronymy SPARQL Database Server	C++	[www.meronymy.com www.meronymy.com]	
Parliament	Java, C++	[parliament.semwebcentral.org parliament.semwebcentral.org]	

Pointrel System	Java, Python	sourceforge.net/projects/pointrel [13]	
RAP	PHP	www4.wiwiss.fu-berlin.de/bizer/rdfapi [14]	
RDF::Core	Perl	search.cpan.org/dist/RDF-Core [15]	
RDF::Trine	Perl	[www.perlrdf.org www.perlrdf.org]	
RDF-3X	C++	www.mpi-inf.mpg.de/~neumann/rdf3x [16]	
RDFBroker	Java	[rdfbroker.opendfki.de rdfbroker.opendfki.de]	
Redland	C	[librdf.org librdf.org]	
RedStore	C	www.aelius.com/njh/redstore [17]	
Semantics Platform	C#	[www.intellidimension.com www.intellidimension.com]	
SemWeb-DotNet	C#	razor.occams.info/code/semweb [18]	
Sesame	Java	[www.openrdf.org www.openrdf.org]	BSD-style license
Soprano	C++	[soprano.sourceforge.net soprano.sourceforge.net]	
Stardog	Java	[stardog.com stardog.com]	
StrixDB	C++, Lua	[www.strixdb.com www.strixdb.com]	
SwiftOWLIM	Java	www.ontotext.com/owlim [9]	
Virtuoso	C	[virtuoso.openlinksw.com virtuoso.openlinksw.com]	
YARS	Java	sw.deri.org/2004/06/yars [19]	
Smart-M3	Python, Java, C, C#	sourceforge.net/projects/smart-m3 [20]	

Technical overview

The following table is an overview triplestores, their technical implementation, support for the SPARQL World Wide Web Consortium (W3C) recommendations, and available application programming interfaces (API).

Solution Name	Internal storage method	SPARQL support	SPARQL/Update support	SPARQL Protocol Endpoint	Supported API's
AllegroGraph	Graph	√	√	√	For most modern programming languages
RDF API for PHP	3rd party	√			PHP
ARQ	3rd party	√	√		Java
Sesame 2	3rd party	√			Java
RDF::Query	3rd party	√			Perl
Twinql	3rd party	√			Lisp
SPARQL Engine	3rd party	√			Java
KAON2	3rd party	√			Java
Pellet	3rd party	√			Java
Corese	3rd party	√			Java
OpenLink Virtuoso	Relational	√	√	√	For most modern programming languages

Ontotext OWLIM	3rd party	√	√	√	Java
ARC2	3rd party	√	√	√	PHP
D2R Server	3rd party	√	√	√	Java
Open Anzo	3rd party	√		√	Java, JavaScript, .NET Framework
BrightstarDB	Graph data model in Heap file	√			.NET Framework or Web Service
Hercules	Stored in web browser	√			JavaScript
4store	Triplestore	√	√	√	Command line only
StrixDB	Triplestore	√	√	√	Lua
OntoBroker	Triplestore	√	√	√	Java
BigData	Triplestore	√			Java
Dydra	Graph database in the cloud SaaS	√	√	√	REST API
Jena	Tuple store	√	√	√	Java
Mulgara	3rd party	√			Java or REST API
Oracle DB Enterprise Ed.	Object-relational	√	√	√	For most modern programming languages
Parliament	Triplestore	√	√	√	Java or C++
Pointrel	Triplestore				Python
RAP	In-memory triplestore or heap file	√			PHP
RDF-3X	Triplestore	√			Command line only
RDFBroker	3rd party				Java
Redland, Redstore	3rd party	√	√	√	C
Intellidimension Semantics Platform 2.0	3rd party	√			.NET Framework
SemWeb.NET	3rd party	√		√	.NET Framework
Soprano	3rd party				C++
Stardog	3rd party	√		√	Java, Groovy
YARS	3rd party				HTTP, JDBC

See also

- Freebase, uses a triplestore called graphd.[21]
- Named graphs

References

[1] TripleStore (http://www.w3.org/2001/sw/Europe/events/20031113-storage/positions/rusher.html), Jack Rusher, Semantic Web Advanced Development for Europe (SWAD-Europe), Workshop on Semantic Web Storage and Retrieval - Position Papers

[2] Tom Ilube (2007-11-30), *Semantic Technologies Really Do Pay Off* (http://www.semanticuniverse.com/articles-semantic-technologies-really-do-pay.html), Semantic Universe,

[3] Lehigh University Triplestore Benchmark (http://swat.cse.lehigh.edu/projects/lubm/)

[4] US 2003145022 (http://worldwide.espacenet.com/textdoc?DB=EPODOC&IDX=US2003145022) Storage and Management of
     Semi-structured Data (Use of SQL relational databases as an RDF triple store), 2003

[5] Broekstra, Jeen (19 September, 2007). "The importance of SPARQL can not be overestimated" (http://www.semantic-web.at/1.36.
     resource.90.jeen-broekstra-x22-the-importance-of-sparql-can-not-be-overestimated-x22.htm). .

[6] http://www.aktors.org/technologies/3store

[7] http://4store.org/trac/wiki/5store

[8] http://www.franz.com/agraph/allegrograph

[9] http://www.ontotext.com/owlim

[10] http://incubator.apache.org/jena/

[11] http://www.ontoprise.de/en/home/products/ontobroker

[12] http://www.oracle.com/technetwork/database/options/semantic-tech/whatsnew

[13] http://sourceforge.net/projects/pointrel

[14] http://www4.wiwiss.fu-berlin.de/bizer/rdfapi

[15] http://search.cpan.org/dist/RDF-Core

[16] http://www.mpi-inf.mpg.de/~neumann/rdf3x

[17] http://www.aelius.com/njh/redstore

[18] http://razor.occams.info/code/semweb

[19] http://sw.deri.org/2004/06/yars

[20] http://sourceforge.net/projects/smart-m3

[21] "a-brief-tour-of-graphd" (http://blog.freebase.com/2008/04/09/a-brief-tour-of-graphd/). . Retrieved 2009-07-08.

External links

- A list of large triplestores (http://esw.w3.org/topic/LargeTripleStores)
- Lehigh University Benchmark (LUBM) (http://swat.cse.lehigh.edu/projects/lubm/)
- Semantic Systems Biology (http://www.semantic-systems-biology.org)
- ARC's RDF Store (https://github.com/semsol/arc2/wiki) is built using PHP with MySQL as the backend for
  the triplestore. It also provides a SPARQL endpoint for access and updating of stored triples.
- How RDF Databases Differ from Other NoSQL Solutions (http://blog.datagraph.org/2010/04/rdf-nosql-diff)
- W3C SPARQL Working Group (http://www.w3.org/2001/sw/DataAccess/), was RDF Data Access Working
  Group
- SPARQL Query language (http://www.w3.org/TR/rdf-sparql-query/)
- SPARQL Protocol (http://www.w3.org/TR/rdf-sparql-protocol/)
- SPARQL 1.1 Update (http://www.w3.org/TR/sparql11-update/) Working Draft from W3C SPARQL
  Working Group

Relational_database

A **relational database** is a collection of data items organized as a set of formally-described tables from which data can be accessed easily. A relation database is created using the relational model. The software used in a relational database is called a relational database management system (RDBMS). A relational database is the predominant choice in storing data, over other models like the hierarchical database model or the network model. For example DBMS includes the theritical part that

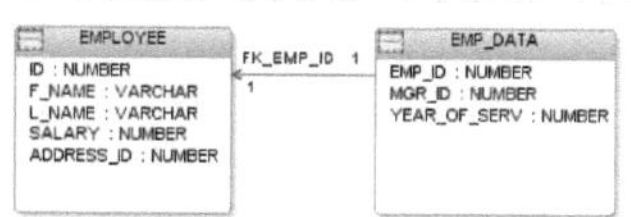

A visual diagram showing the relationship between the two tables, as indicated by the arrow

how data is stored in a table. It does not relates tables with another. While RDBMS is the procedural way that includes SQL syntaxes for relating tables with another and handling data stored in the tables.

Contents

Terminology

The term *relational database* was originally defined by and is attributed to Edgar Codd at IBM Almaden Research Center in 1970.[1]

Relational database theory uses a set of mathematical terms, which are roughly equivalent to SQL database terminology. The table below summarizes some of the most important relational database terms and their SQL database equivalents.

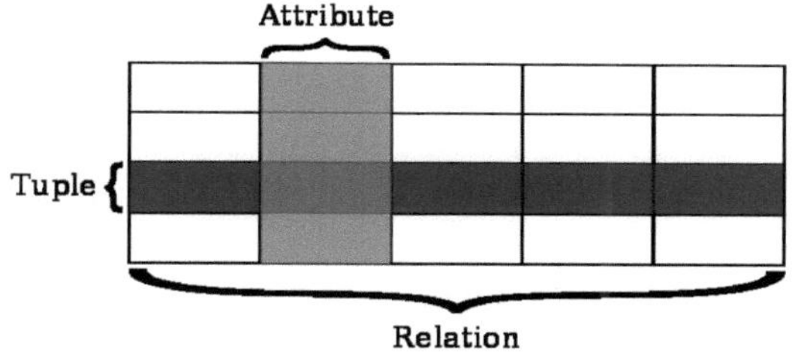

Relational database terminology.

Relational term	SQL equivalent
relation, base relvar	table
derived relvar	view, query result, result set
tuple	row
attribute	column

Relations or Tables

A *relation* is defined as a set of tuples that have the same attributes. A tuple usually represents an object and information about that object. Objects are typically physical objects or concepts. A relation is usually described as a table, which is organized into rows and columns. All the data referenced by an attribute are in the same domain and conform to the same constraints.

The relational model specifies that the tuples of a relation have no specific order and that the tuples, in turn, impose no order on the attributes. Applications access data by specifying queries, which use operations such as *select* to identify tuples, *project* to identify attributes, and *join* to combine relations. Relations can be modified using the *insert*, *delete*, and *update* operators. New tuples can supply explicit values or be derived from a query. Similarly, queries identify tuples for updating or deleting. It is necessary for each tuple of a relation to be uniquely identifiable by some combination (one or more) of its attribute values. This combination is referred to as the primary key.

Base and derived relations

In a relational database, all data are stored and accessed via relations. Relations that store data are called "base relations", and in implementations are called "tables". Other relations do not store data, but are computed by applying relational operations to other relations. These relations are sometimes called "derived relations". In implementations these are called "views" or "queries". Derived relations are convenient in that though they may grab information from several relations, they act as a single relation. Also, derived relations can be used as an abstraction layer.

Domain

A domain describes the set of possible values for a given attribute, and can be considered a constraint on the value of the attribute. Mathematically, attaching a domain to an attribute means that any value for the attribute must be an element of the specified set.

The character data value 'ABC', for instance, is not in the integer domain. The integer value 123, satisfies the domain constraint.

Constraints

Constraints make it possible to further restrict the domain of an attribute. For instance, a constraint can restrict a given integer attribute to values between 1 and 10. Constraints provide one method of implementing business rules in the database. SQL implements constraint functionality in the form of check constraints.

Constraints restrict the data that can be stored in relations. These are usually defined using expressions that result in a boolean value, indicating whether or not the data satisfies the constraint. Constraints can apply to single attributes, to a tuple (restricting combinations of attributes) or to an entire relation.

Since every attribute has an associated domain, there are constraints (**domain constraints**). The two principal rules for the relational model are known as **entity integrity** and **referential integrity**. ("Referential integrity is the state in which all values of all foreign keys are valid. Referential integrity is based on entity integrity. Entity integrity requires that each entity have a unique key. For example, if every row in a table represents relationships for a unique entity, the table should have one column or a set of columns that provides a unique identifier for the rows of the table. This column (or set of columns) is called the parent key of the table. To ensure that the parent key does not contain duplicate values, a unique index must be defined on the column or columns that constitute the parent key. Defining the parent key is called entity integrity")

Primary keys

A primary key uniquely defines a relationship within a database. In order for an attribute to be a good primary key it must not repeat. While natural attributes are sometimes good primary keys, surrogate keys are often used instead. A surrogate key is an artificial attribute assigned to an object which uniquely identifies it (for instance, in a table of information about students at a school they might all be assigned a student ID in order to differentiate them). The surrogate key has no intrinsic (inherent) meaning, but rather is useful through its ability to uniquely identify a tuple.

Another common occurrence, especially in regards to N:M cardinality is the composite key. A composite key is a key made up of two or more attributes within a table that (together) uniquely identify a record. (For example, in a database relating students, teachers, and classes. Classes *could* be uniquely identified by a composite key of their room number and time slot, since no other class could have exactly the same combination of attributes. In fact, use of a composite key such as this can be a form of data verification, albeit a weak one.)

Foreign key

A foreign key is a field in a relational table that matches the primary key column of another table. The foreign key can be used to cross-reference tables. Foreign keys need not have unique values in the referencing relation. Foreign keys effectively use the values of attributes in the referenced relation to restrict the domain of one or more attributes in the referencing relation.

A foreign key could be described formally as: "For all tuples in the referencing relation projected over the referencing attributes, there must exist a tuple in the referenced relation projected over those same attributes such that the values in each of the referencing attributes match the corresponding values in the referenced attributes."

Stored procedures

A stored procedure is executable code that is associated with, and generally stored in, the database. Stored procedures usually collect and customize common operations, like inserting a tuple into a relation, gathering statistical information about usage patterns, or encapsulating complex business logic and calculations. Frequently they are used as an application programming interface (API) for security or simplicity. Implementations of stored procedures on SQL DBMSs often allow developers to take advantage of procedural extensions (often vendor-specific) to the standard declarative SQL syntax.

Stored procedures are not part of the relational database model, but all commercial implementations include them.

Index

An index is one way of providing quicker access to data. Indices can be created on any combination of attributes on a relation. Queries that filter using those attributes can find matching tuples randomly using the index, without having to check each tuple in turn. This is analogous to using the index of a book to go directly to the page on which the information you are looking for is found i.e. you do not have to read the entire book to find what you are looking for. Relational databases typically supply multiple indexing techniques, each of which is optimal for some combination of data distribution, relation size, and typical access pattern. Indices are usually implemented via B+ trees, R-trees, and bitmaps.

Indices are usually not considered part of the database, as they are considered an implementation detail, though indices are usually maintained by the same group that maintains the other parts of the database. It should be noted that use of efficient indexes on both primary and foreign keys can dramatically improve query performance. This is because B-tree indexes result in query times proportional to $\log(n)$ where N is the number of rows in a table and hash indexes result in constant time queries (no size dependency so long as the relevant part of the index fits into memory).

Relational operations

Queries made against the relational database, and the derived relvars in the database are expressed in a relational calculus or a relational algebra. In his original relational algebra, Codd introduced eight relational operators in two groups of four operators each. The first four operators were based on the traditional mathematical set operations:

- The union operator combines the tuples of two relations and removes all duplicate tuples from the result. The relational union operator is equivalent to the SQL UNION operator.
- The intersection operator produces the set of tuples that two relations share in common. Intersection is implemented in SQL in the form of the INTERSECT operator.
- The difference operator acts on two relations and produces the set of tuples from the first relation that do not exist in the second relation. Difference is implemented in SQL in the form of the EXCEPT or MINUS operator.
- The cartesian product of two relations is a join that is not restricted by any criteria, resulting in every tuple of the first relation being matched with every tuple of the second relation. The cartesian product is implemented in SQL as the CROSS JOIN join operator.

The remaining operators proposed by Codd involve special operations specific to relational databases:

- The selection, or restriction, operation retrieves tuples from a relation, limiting the results to only those that meet a specific criteria, i.e. a subset in terms of set theory. The SQL equivalent of selection is the SELECT query statement with a WHERE clause.
- The projection operation extracts only the specified attributes from a tuple or set of tuples.
- The join operation defined for relational databases is often referred to as a natural join. In this type of join, two relations are connected by their common attributes. SQL's approximation of a natural join is the INNER JOIN join operator.
- The relational division operation is a slightly more complex operation, which involves essentially using the tuples of one relation (the dividend) to partition a second relation (the divisor). The relational division operator is effectively the opposite of the cartesian product operator (hence the name).

Other operators have been introduced or proposed since Codd's introduction of the original eight including relational comparison operators and extensions that offer support for nesting and hierarchical data, among others.

Normalization

Normalization was first proposed by Codd as an integral part of the relational model. It encompasses a set of procedures designed to eliminate nonsimple domains (non-atomic values) and the redundancy (duplication) of data, which in turn prevents data manipulation anomalies and loss of data integrity. The most common forms of normalization applied to databases are called the normal forms. Normalization trades reducing redundancy for increased information entropy. Normalization is criticised because it increases complexity and processing overhead required to join multiple tables representing what are conceptually a single item .

Relational database management systems

Relational databases, as implemented in relational database management systems, have become a predominant choice for the storage of information in new databases used for financial records, manufacturing and logistical information, personnel data and much more. Relational databases have often replaced legacy hierarchical databases and network databases because they are easier to understand and use, even though they are much less efficient. As computer power has increased, the inefficiencies of relational databases, which made them impractical in earlier times, have been outweighed by their ease of use. However, relational databases have been challenged by Object Databases, which were introduced in an attempt to address the object-relational impedance mismatch in relational database, and XML databases.

The three leading commercial relational database vendors are Oracle, Microsoft, and IBM.[2] The three leading open source implementations are MySQL, PostgreSQL, and SQLite. Amazon Relational Database Service is a database as a service offering MySQL and Oracle database engines.

Watermarking for Relational Databases

Digital watermarking for relational databases emerged as a candidate solution to provide copyright protection, tamper detection, traitor tracing, maintaining integrity of relational data. Many watermarking techniques have been proposed in the literature to address these purposes.

Notes

[1] Codd, E.F. (1970). "A Relational Model of Data for Large Shared Data Banks". *Communications of the ACM* **13** (6): 377–387. doi:10.1145/362384.362685.

[2] Gartner Says Worldwide Relational Database Market Increased 14 Percent in 2006 (http://www.gartner.com/it/page.jsp?id=507466), includes revenue estimates for leading database companies

References

* Raju Halder, Shantanu Pal, and Agostino Cortesi (2010). "Watermarking Techniques for Relational Databases: Survey, Classification and Comparison", *The Journal of Universal Computer Science*, vol 16(21), pp. 3164-3190, 2010.
* Difference between dbms and rdbms. In Scribd. Retrieved April 5, 2012, from http://www.scribd.com/ mandeepdhaliwal/d/37351788-22161565-Difference-Between-Dbms-and-Rdbms

AllegroGraph

Developer(s)	Franz, Inc.
Stable release	3.3 / February 22, 2010
Operating system	Microsoft Windows (32 and 64-bit), Mac OS X (Intel, 32 and 64-bit), Linux (32 and 64-bit), FreeBSD, Solaris (x64)
License	Proprietary commercial software
Website	Franz, Inc. [1]

AllegroGraph[2] is a closed source Graph database, an emerging category of databases. In contrast with a Relational database, a graph database considers each stored item to have any number of relationships. These relationships can be viewed as links, which together form a network, or graph. AllegroGraph is designed to store RDF tuples, a standard format for Linked Data. A custom browser, Gruff, is available for viewing the graph.

AllegroGraph is currently in use in Open source projects,[3] , commercial projects[4] [5] [6] and Department of Defense projects[7] . It is also the storage component for the TwitLogic project[8] that is bringing the Semantic Web to Twitter data.

Implementation

AllegroGraph was developed to meet W3C standards for the Resource Description Framework, so it is properly considered an RDF Database. It is a reference implementation for the SPARQL protocol[9] . SPARQL is a standard query language for linked data, serving the same purposes for RDF databases that SQL serves for relational databases.

The company that makes AllegroGraph, Franz, Inc. [1], made its reputation with its Allegro Common Lisp implementation of Common Lisp, a dialect of Lisp (programming language). The functionality of AllegroGraph is made available through a Common Lisp interface.

The first version of AllegroGraph was made available at the end of 2004.

Languages

AllegroGraph has client interfaces for Java, Python, Ruby, Perl, C#, Clojure, and Common Lisp. The product is available for Windows, Linux, and Mac OS X platforms, supporting 32 or 64 bits.

AllegroGraph includes an implementation of Prolog based on the implementation developed by Peter Norvig in Paradigms of Artificial Intelligence Programming.[10]

References

[1] http://www.franz.com
[2] Dr. Dobbs (http://www.drdobbs.com/web-development/199001127)
[3] DBPedia Germany (http://www.corporate-semantic-web.de/reader/items/
      dbpedia-deutschland-10-release-the-german-part-of-the-wikipedia-for-machines.html)
[4] GenomeWeb-Pfizer Article (http://www.genomeweb.com/informatics/
      pfizer-partners-io-franz-semantic-proof-concept-build-bridges-between-data-resou)
[5] Eli Lilly Project Presentation (http://www.iscb.org/cms_addon/conferences/cshals2009/presentations/GudivadaCFeb09.pdf)
[6] Making a Semantic Web Business Case at Pfizer (http://www.semanticweb.com/news/
      making_a_semantic_web_business_case_at_pfizer_161731.asp)
[7] Contributions to a Semantically Based Intelligence Analysis Enterprise Workflow System (http://c4i.gmu.edu/OIC09/papers/
      OIC2009_4_SchragEtAll.pdf)
[8] TwitLogic Paper (http://events.linkeddata.org/ldow2010/papers/ldow2010_paper16.pdf)
[9] SPARQL Protocol Implementation Report (http://www.w3.org/2001/sw/DataAccess/impl-report-protocol)

[10] Allegro Prolog (http://www.franz.com/agraph/support/documentation/3.2/prolog-tutorial.html)

External links

- Official website (http://http://www.franz.com/agraph/allegrograph)
- Mark Watson's books (http://www.markwatson.com) (see Open Content > Practical Semantic Web Programming)

Article Sources and Contributors

Graph_database *Source*: http://en.wikipedia.org/w/index.php?title=Graph_database *Contributors*: 0x24a537r9, Agavenwurm, Aglnl, Ahzf, Ajmagnifico, Aldonline, Andrearatto, Bolerio, Bunnyhop11, Cnorvell, Colinniu, Crcsmnky, DamarisC, Danim, Espeed, Ffangs, Fraktalek, Frap, Freshnfruity, Germanviscuso, Giftlite, J12t, JakobVoss, Jncraton, Jni, Jonik, Lguzenda, Luisbargu, MacTed, Magnuschr, Miami33139, Michael A. White, Morphh, MuffledThud, Nawroth, Pelister, Pholding, Praveensripati, ProfessorBaltasar, RecaiAlkan, RichMorin, SamJohnston, Stybn, Syhuang1988, TTJDenman, Tgrota, Thoughtpuzzle, Tuhl, Yanivby, 62 anonymous edits

Graph_(abstract_data_type) *Source*: http://en.wikipedia.org/w/index.php?title=Graph_%28abstract_data_type%29 *Contributors*: 31stCenturyMatt, A Aleg, Aaronzat, Alink, Andreas Kaufmann, Any Key, AvicAWB, Avoided, Bluebusy, Booyabazooka, Bruyninc, C4Cypher, Chochopk, Chrisholland, Cooldudefx, Cybercobra, David Eppstein, Dcoetzee, Dysprosia, Epimethius, FedericoMenaQuintero, Gallando, Giftlite, Gmelli, Graphicalx, Gvanrossum, Hariva, Hobsonlane, Jojit fb, Jon Awbrey, JonHarder, Jorge Stolfi, Juliancolton, Kate4341, Kazubon, Kbrose, KellyCoinGuy, Kendrick Hang, Klortho, KristjanJonasson, Labraun90, Liao, Max Terry, NerdyNSK, Nmz787, Obradovic Goran, Ovi 1, POnc, Pbirnie, Pieleric, R. S. Shaw, RG2, Rabarberski, Rborrego, Rd232, Rhanekom, Ruud Koot, Sae1962, Saimhe, Salix alba, ScaledLizard, SimonFuhrmann, Simonfairfax, SiobhanHansa, Skippydo, Stphung, TFloto, Timwi, Tyir, Zoicon5, ZorroIII, ZweiOhren, 128 anonymous edits

Database *Source*: http://en.wikipedia.org/w/index.php?title=Database *Contributors*: *drew, 05winsjp, 10285658sdsaa, 10metreh, 110808028 amol, 16@r, 206.31.111.xxx, 25or6to4, 28421u2232nfenfcenc, 28nebraska, 2D, 4twenty42o, 65.10.163.xxx, APH, Aaron Brenneman, Abhikumar1995, Addihockey10, Aditya gopal3, Admfirepanther, Adrian J. Hunter, Aepanico, Afluegel, Ahodgkinson, Ahoerstemeier, Ahy1, Aitias, Aj.robin, Akamad, Al Wiseman, Alain Amiouni, Alansohn, Alasdair, Ale jrb, Allan McInnes, Allecher, Alpha Quadrant (alt), Alphax, Alzpp, Amaraiel, Amd628, Anders Torlind, Andonic, Andre Engels, Andrewferrier, AndriuZ, Angela, Anikingos, AnjaliSinha, AnmaFinotera, Ann Stouter, AnonUser, Anonymous Dissident, Antandrus, Antrax, Apparition11, Arbitrarily0, Arcann, Argon233, Arjun01, Armen1304, ArnoLagrange, Arthena, Arved, ArwinJ, Asyndeton, AtheWeatherman, Atkinsdc, AutumnSnow, Avenged Eightfold, AwamerT, Ayecee, AzaToth, Baa, Babbling.Brook, Barneca, Bbatsell, Bblank, Bcartolo, Bcontins, Beeblebrox, Beetstra, Beland, Ben Ben, Ben-Zin, Benni39, Bentogoa, Bernd in Japan, Beta M, Betterusername, Bharath357, Bjcubsfan, Bkhouser, Blanchardb, BlindEagle, Blood Red Sandman, BluCreator, Bluemask, Bluerocket, BobStepno, Bobblewik, Bogdangiusca, Bogey97, Boing! said Zebedee, Bongwarrior, Bowlderizer, Branzman, Brick Thrower, BrokenSphere, BryanG, Btilm, Bubba hotep, Burner0718, Buzzimu, Bwhynot14, C12H22O11, CIreland, COMPFUNK2, CableCat, Calabe1992, Call me Bubba, Calliopejen1, Caltas, Calutuigor, Cambapp, Cammo33, Camw, Can't sleep, clown will eat me, CanisRufus, Canterbury Tail, Cantras, Capricorn42, Captain-n00dle, Captain-tucker, Carbonite, CardinalDan, Caster23, CasualVisitor, Cavanagh, Cenarium, CesarB, Cevalsi, Ceyjan, Chaojoker, Chester Markel, Childzy, Chirpy, Chocolateboy, ChorizoLasagna, Chrax, Chris 73, Chris G, Chrislk02, Christophe.billiottet, Chriswiki, Chtuw, Chuckhoffmann, Chuunen Baka, Clarince63, Clark89, Click23, Closedmouth, Colindolly, Colonies Chris, Cometstyles, Commander Keane, Comps, Constructive, Conversion script, Courcelles, Cpereyra, Cpl Syx, Cpuwhiz11, Craftyminion, Craig Stuntz, Crashdown, Credema, Crucis, Cryptic, Culverin, Cyan, Cybercobra, Cyberjoac, CynicalMe, D. Recorder, DARTH SIDIOUS 2, DEddy, DFS454, DJ Clayworth, DVD R W, DVdm, DamnRandall, Dan100, Dancayta, Dancter, Danhash, Daniel.Cardenas, DanielCD, Danieljamesscott, Danim, Dart88, Darth Mike, Darth Panda, Darthvader023, Davewild, David Fuchs, David0811, Dbates1999, Dbfirs, DePiep, Dead3y3, DeadEyeArrow, DeadlyAssassin, Deathlaser, Decrease789, DeirdreGerhardt, Denisarona, DerBorg, DerHexer, Deville, Dgw, Diamondland, DigitalEnthusiast, Discospinster, Djordjes, Djsasso, Dkastner, Doc glasgow, Doddsy1993, Dogposter, Donama, Doniago, DougBarry, Dougofborg, Doulos Christos, Dreadstar, Dreamyshade, Drivenapart, Drumroll99, Duyanfang, Dwolt, Dysepsion, E23, Eagleal, Earlypsychosis, EarthPerson, EastTN, Echartre, Edgar181, Edivorce, Edward, Eeekster, Ejrrjs, ElKevbo, Elwikipedista, Epbr123, Era7bd, Eric Bekins, Eric Burnett, Ericlaw02, Erikrj, Escape Orbit, Etxrge, EugeneZelenko, Everyking, Evildeathmath, Excirial, Exor674, Explicit, Ezeu, FFGeyer, Fang Aili, FatalError, Favonian, Feedmecereal, FetchcommsAWB, Feydey, Fieldday-sunday, Filx, Finlay McWalter, Flewis, Flubeca, Fluffernutter, FlyingToaster, Fooker69, Foxfax555, Frankman, Franky21, Franl, Fratrep, Frsparrow, Fubar Obfusco, Furrykef, Fuzzie, Fæ, G12kid, GDonato, GHe, GLaDOS, Gadfium, Gail, Garyzx, Giftlite, Ginsengbomb, Girl2k, Gishac, Glacialfox, GlenPeterson, GnuDoyng, Gogo Dodo, GoingBatty, Gonfus, Gozzy345, Graeme Bartlett, GraemeL, Graham87, GrayFullbuster, GregWPhoto, Gregfitzy, GregorB, Grim23, Grstain, Gsallis, Gscshoyru, Gwizard, Gzkn, Haakon, Hadal, HaeB, Hamtechperson, Hankhuck, HappyInGeneral, Harej, Hasek is the best, HeliXx, Helixblue, Helloher, HexaChord, Heymid, HeysimOn, Hotstaff, Hugsandy, Huntthetroll, Hurricane111, HybridBoy, Hydrogen Iodide, IElonex!, Iced Kola, Igoldste, Imfargo, Imnotminkus, Imran, Informatwr, Insineratehymn, Inspector 34, Ironman5247, Isfisk, Itafran2010, ItsZippy, Ixfd64, J.delanoy, JCLately, JForget, JLaTondre, JMRyan, Ja 62, JaGa, Jab843, Jackacon, JamesBWatson, Jan1nad, Jasimab, Jasper Deng, Jauerback, Javert, Jaxl, Jb-adder, Jclemens, Jdlambert, JeffTan, JeffreyYasskin, Jennavecia, JephapE, Jerome Charles Potts, Jhfireboy, Jk2q3jrklse, Jmanigold, Jni, JoanneB, Joel7687, John Vandenberg, John of Reading, Johnuniq, Jojalozzo, Jonathan Webley, JonathanFreed, Jonearles, Jonwynne, Johnpowell, Joshwa1234567890, Journalist, Jstaniek, Jvhertum, Jwoodger, Jwy, KILLERKEA23, Kanonkas, Karlhahn, Karmafist, Katalaveno, Keenan Pepper, Keilana, Kekekecakes, Kellyk99, Kenny sh, Kevins, KeyStroke, Khoikhoi, Kiand, Kimberly ayoma, Kimera Kat, King of Hearts, Kingius, Kingpin13, Kingsleyldehen, Kivar2, Kkailas, Knbanker, Koavf, Komal.Ar, KoshVorlon, KotetsuKat, Kozmando, Kraftlos, Krashlandon, Kslays, Kubigula, Kukini, Kunaldeo, Kungfuadam, Kuru, Kushal one, Kvasilev, Kwiki, KyraVixen, Kzzl, L Kensington, LC, LaosLos, Larsinio, Latka, Leaderofearth, Leandrod, LeaveSleaves, LeeHam2007, Leonnicholls07, LessHeard vanU, Levin, Levin Carsten, Lexo, Lflores92201, Lfstevens, Lguzenda, Lights, LindaEllen, Lingliu07, Lingwitt, Linkspamremover, LittleOldMe, LittleWink, Llyntegid, Lod, Logan, Lotje, Lovefamosos, Lovelac7, Lowellian, Lradrama, Lsschwar, LuK3, Lucyin, Luizfsc, Luna Santin, M.badnjki, M4gnum0n, MBisanz, MECiAf., MER-C, Madhava 1947, Majorly, Mandarax, Manikandan 2030, Mannafredo, Marasmusine, Mark Renier, MarkSutton, MartinSpamer, Materialscientist, Mathewforyou, Mato, Matthewrbowker, Matticus78, Mattisse, May18, Maury Markowitz, Max Naylor, Maxferrario, Maxime.Debosschere, Maxmarengo, Mayur, Mazca, Mboverload, Mdd, Meaghan, Megatronium, Melucky2getu, Mentifisto, Mephistophelian, Mercy11, Methnor, Mhkay, Michael Hardy, Michael Slone, Microchip08, Mike Dillon, Mike Rosoft, Mike Schwartz, MikeSy, Mikeblas, Mikey180791, MilerWhite, Millermk90, Milo99, Mindmatrix, Minimac, Minna Sora no Shita, Mkeranat, Moreschi, Morwen, MrNoblet, Mspraveen, Mugaliens, Mulad, Mumonkan, Mushroom, Mxn, N1RK4UDSK714, N25696, NAHID, NSR, Nafclark, Namlemez, Nanshu, NathanBeach, NawlinWiki, NetManage, Netizen, NewEnglandYankee, Ngpd, Nick, Nicoosuna, Niteowlneils, Nk, Noah Salzman, Noldoaran, Northamerica1000, Northernhenge, Nsaa, Nurg, Ocaasi, Oda Mari, Odavy, Ohka-, Oho1, Oli Filth, Olinga, OllieFury, OnePt618, OrgasGirl, Oroso, OverlordQ, PJM, PaePae, Pak21, Parzi, PatrikR, Paul August, Paul Drye, Paul E Ester, Paul Foxworthy, Paulinho28, Pcb21, Pdcook, Peashy, Pee Tern, PeeAeMKay, Pengo, PeregrineAY, Peruvianllama, Peter Karlsen, Peter.C, Pgk, Phantomsteve, Pharaoh of the Wizards, Phearlez, PhilKnight, Philip Trueman, Philippe, Phoenix-wiki, Piano non troppo, Pillefj, Pingveno, Pinkadelica, Pjoef, Plrk, Pnm, Poeloq, Pol098, Poor Yorick, Poterxu, Praba tuty, Prari, Prashanthns, PrePress, Preet91119, Proofreader77, Prunesqualer, Psaajid, Psb777, Puchiko, Pvjohnson, Pyfan, Quadell, Qwertykris, Qwyrxian, Qxz, R'n'B, RIH-V, RadioFan, RadioKirk, Railgun, Rakeki, Ravinjit, RayGates, RayMetz100, RazorXX8, Rdsmith4, Reaper Eternal, Refactored, Regancy42, Reidh21234, Rettetast, RexNL, Rhobite, Rich Farmbrough, Ricky81682, Ringbang, Rishu arora11, Riverraisin, Rj Haseeb, Rjwilmsi, Robert Merkel, Robert Skyhawk, Robocoder, Robth, Romanm, Rotanagol, Rothwellisretarded, Roux, Rursus, Ruud Koot, Ryager, Ryanslater, Ryanslater2, Ryulong, S.K., SAE1962, SDSWIKI, SJP, SWAdair, Sae1962, Saiken79, Salvio giuliano, Sam Barsoom, Sam Korn, SamJohnston, Samir, Sandman, Sango123, Sarchand, SarekOfVulcan, SatuSuro, Saturdayswiki, Savh, ScMeGr, Sceptre, Seanust 1, Seaphoto, SebastianHelm, Serketan, Several Pending, Sewebster, Shadowseas, Sheeana, Shipmaster, Shirulashem, Siebren, Silly rabbit, Simeon, Simetrical, SimonMorgan, Sinitaku, Sir Nicholas de Mimsy-Porpington, Sissi's bd, Siteobserver, Sjakkalle, Sjc, Skybrian, Slakr, Sleske, SnoFox, Somchai1029, Sonett72, Sonia, Soosed, Soumark, SpK, Spartaz, Spazure, Spdegabrielle, SpikeTorontoRCP, SpuriousQ, Srdju001, Srikeit, Ssd, StaticVision, Stdazi, Stephen Gilbert, Stevertigo, Stifle, Stirling Newberry, Storm Rider, Strongsauce, Stuhacking, Sucker666, Sudarevic, Suffusion of Yellow, SuperHamster, Supertouch, Supreme Deliciousness, Supten, SwisterTwister, SymlynX, Sythy2, Tabletop, Tablizer, TakuyaMurata, TalkyLemon, Tasc, Tazmaniacs, Th1rt3en, Thatperson, The Anome, The Thing That Should Not Be, The Wiki Octopus, The wub, TheGrimReaper NS, TheNewPhobia, Thedjatclubrock, Thehulkmonster, Theimmaculatechemist, Theodolite, Theory of deadman, Thingg, Think outside the box, Thinktdub, Thomasryno, ThumbFinger, Thumperward, Tictacsir, Tide rolls, Tim Q. Wells, TimBentley, TittoAssini, Tobias Bergemann, Tomatronster, Tonydent, Tpbradbury, Treekids, TrentonLipscomb, Trevor MacInnis, Triwbe, Troels Arvin, Trusilver, Tualha, Tudorol, Tuhl, Turlo Lomon, Turnstep, Twebby, Twelvethirteen, TwistOfCain, Twsx, UberScienceNerd, Ubiq, Ugebgroup8, Ulric1313, Ultraexactzz, Uncle Dick, Unyoyega, VNeumann, Vary, Velella, Versus22, Veryprettyfish, Vespristiano, Victor falk, Vikreykja, Vipinhari, Vishnava, Visor, Vivacewwxu, VoxLuna, Vrenator, W mccall, WOSlinker, Waggers, Waveguy, Wavelength, Weetoddid, Welsh, Werdna, Widefox, Wifione, Wik, Wiki alf, Wiki tiki tr, Wikidrone, Wikipelli, WikiuserNI, Willking1979, Wimt, Windsok, Winterst, Wipe, Wmahan, Woohookitty, Woseph, Writeread82, Wulfila, Wwmbes, Wya 7890, Xhelllox, Xin0427, Yossman007, ZenerV, Zhenqinli, Zhou Yu, Zipircik, Zippanova, ZooPro, Zro, Zundark, Zzuuzz, Σ, فش ابل, لبقع يق, 2723 anonymous edits

Computer_data_storage *Source*: http://en.wikipedia.org/w/index.php?title=Computer_data_storage *Contributors*: AThing, Aapo Laitinen, Aaron Schulz, Abstract, Abune, Achraf52, Acroterion, AdjustShift, Ahoerstemeier, Aiken drum, Ajustis, Alansohn, Alaphent, Aldie, Algotime, Alpha Quadrant (alt), Altenmann, Ancheta Wis, Andrew Hampe, Andrewpmk, Anfeardar, Anghammarad, Anigma10363, Archer7, Arthena, Arthuralee, Ary29, Atif.t2, Austinmurphy, Aveilleux, B jonas, Bact, Bansipatel, Beetstra, Ben.c.roberts, BenFrantzDale, Beyond silence, BigCow, Bitbut, BlastOBunter42, Bluerasberry, Bobblewik, Bobo192, Borgx, Brad101, Brookie, Bsadowski1, CBDunkerson, Callmejosh, Caltas, Calvin 1998, Canadian-Bacon, CanisRufus, Celebere, Ceros, Ch Th Jo, Channabankapur, Christopher140691, Chuq, Ciphers, ClaireEvans, Clitton01, Cometstyles, Conversion script, Cooltude, Courcelles, CoyneT, Cpritchett42, Cuckooman4, Cyanoa Crylate, Cybercobra, DARTH SIDIOUS 2, DPdH, DVD R W, Damieng, Darth Panda, David Biddulph, David44357, Dcljr, Denniss, Discospinster, Dmooney, Dontdoit, DoubleBlue, Doulos Christos, Dycedarg, Eagleal, Earthlyreason, Eastlaw, Ecemaml, Edward, Eeekster, Elsendero, Emperorbma, Enviroboy, Epolk, Eurobas, Evice, Exagridsystems, Excirial, FT2, Fabartus, Face, Fir0002, Fominf, Fox2030, Frap, Freiberg, Fryed-peach, Funandtrvl, Fuzheado, GB fan, GDonato, GEBStgo, Gadfium, Gaff, Gaius Cornelius, Galoubet, Gamsbart, Giftlite, Gingekerr, Giraffedata, Glen, Glenn, Gokulhraj, Graham87, Guanxi, Gwernol, Haggis, Hagrinas, HappyInGeneral, Helix84, HenkeB, Hovev, Hydrargyrum, Imran, Ixfd64, JCLately, JE, Jacek Kendysz, Jacroe, Jeffrey O. Gustafson, JesseW, Jhfireboy, Jimothytrotter, Johnuniq, Jon.bruce, JonHarder, Josh Parris, Joshua, Joshua Gyamfi, Joshuaneil, Jpbowen, JuJube, Jusdafax, K.Nevelsteen, KJS77, Kaiyuan, Karl-Henner, Katalaveno, Katari88, Kbdank71, Kelly Martin, Kenny sh, Ketsuekigata, Khendon, Kittsville, Kjanos, Kjkolb, Kmg90, Kneepole, KnowledgeOfSelf, Kozuch, Kpacquer, Krashlandon, Kubanczyk, Kungfuadam, Kvng, LX, Leadwind, Lenehey, Lizarddoctor, Loren.wilton, Lowercase Sigma, M1ss1ontomars2k4, MER-C, Mac, Macademe, Mailer diablo, Majorly, Marcan, Mark Foskey, Materialscientist, Matt Britt, Matusz, Maury Markowitz, Meerkate1990, MegaSloth, Memorysuppliers, Mentifisto, Mgoida, Mh234, Michael Hardy, MichaelWattam, Mikeo, Mild Bill Hiccup, Mindmatrix, Minesweeper, Mjscud, Mmxx, Morken, Motor, Mpgenius, Mrmcompserv, Msp786, Muppet, Music Sorter, Mute Linguist, My76Strat, Myanw, Narutolovehinata5, Nate Silva, NawlinWiki, Neelix, NevilleRaymond, NewEnglandYankee, Nialsh, Nightsailor13, Nixdorf, Noommos, Noone, Nuno Tavares, Ogat, Oicumayberight, Onorem, OrgasGirl, Orphan Wiki, Ortisa, Oscarthecat, Oxymoron83, Patrick, Pearle, Peruvianllama, PhilKnight, Philthecow, Piano non troppo, Plugwash, Pne, Pnm, Pokeman, Pol098, Prari, Prashanthns, PrestonH, Professor Magneto, Public Menace, Qwertyas, R. S. Shaw, RTC, Raheel52000, Rama's Arrow, Reaper Eternal, Rebroad, Redmercury82, Reedy, RekishiEJ, Requestion, Rhobite, Rich Farmbrough, RichardF, Rick Sidwell, Ridge Runner, Rigadoun, Rilak, Ronz, RoseParks, RossPatterson, Rror, Rtyq2, RyanCross, Rynsaha, Sam Korn, Santryl, SaturdayNightSpecial, Sav avril,

Sbluen, SchreyP, Sciurinæ, Sfoskett, Shanes, Shawnc, Sheogorath, Sifaka, Signalhead, Slakr, Slightsmile, Smalljim, SoleraTec, Sotdh, SpaceFlight89, Specs112, StaticGull, Stevertigo, Storageman, Surachit, T-bonham, THEN WHO WAS PHONE?, Tannin, Technopilgrim, Thatguyflint, Thaurisil, The Anonymous One, The Thing That Should Not Be, TheBendster, TheSeer, Tiddly Tom, Tide rolls, Tim1357, Tizio, Tobias Bergemann, Tom94022, Tomdo08, Tommy2010, Tubular, Twistednightmare, TzaB, Ultramandk, Uncle Scrooge, Urhixidur, VampWillow, Vectro, Versus22, Vespristiano, Victor, VictorianMutant, ViperSnake151, Vipinhari, Waihorace, Wapcaplet, Warut, Wavelength, Wayne Slam, Welsh, Wernher, Wiki alf, WikiBone, Wikisteve316, Wimt, Wknight94, WojPob, Wombatcat, Woohookitty, WorkingBeaver, Wtmitchell, Wtshymanski, Xqt, Yelyos, Yoosq, Zelikazi, ZeroUm, Zhen Lin, ZimZalaBim, Zoltar0, ZooFari, דוד ש׳, ملاع بوبحم‎, आशिष भटनागर, 730 anonymous edits

Lookup *Source*: http://en.wikipedia.org/w/index.php?title=Lookup *Contributors*: 16@r, Amicron, Brihar73, Cfeet77, Denisarona, Dennislphillips, Frap, Hu12, INVERTED, Jaksmata, Jesser07, Kingpin13, Loadmaster, Mikhus, Mild Bill Hiccup, Ohnoitsjamie, Patrick, Rwwww, S, Samdutton, Tnxman307, Unfree, Wikianon, 13 anonymous edits

Network_model *Source*: http://en.wikipedia.org/w/index.php?title=Network_model *Contributors*: AVB, Aditya, Adrianwn, Anonymous Dissident, Barkeep, BonsaiViking, Brick Thrower, Bucketsofg, Can't sleep, clown will eat me, Capricorn42, Cybercobra, Danim, Darkov, David Eppstein, Dbates1999, DeadEyeArrow, Dnnk, Dpm64, Elwikipedista, Enric Naval, Expensivehat, GermanX, Greentryst, Gurch, Jamelan, Jpbowen, KGasso, Kate, Kbrose, KingsleyIdehen, Krawi, Kuru, Lifebaka, MER-C, Magomaitin, Mange01, Mark Renier, Master of Puppets, Mdd, Meca999, Media lib, Mhkay, Mikeo, Mindmatrix, Nibuod, Nick, Ocrow, Pavel Vozenilek, Petergreer, Phatfish, Phe, Philip Trueman, Pvjohnson, RMFan1, Razorbliss, Rholton, S.K., SJP, ShaunES, Shoujun, Spiritia, Synchronism, The Thing That Should Not Be, Tomrud, Toyota prius 2, Vikreykja, Wj32, Yuriz, ZimZalaBim, 106 anonymous edits

Triplestore *Source*: http://en.wikipedia.org/w/index.php?title=Triplestore *Contributors*: Andy Dingley, Bomazi, BuZZdEE.BuzZ, Cnorvell, Cybercobra, DBooth, Danim, Djlambert, Earle Martin, Enric Naval, Erick.Antezana, FrankTobia, Good Olfactory, Inverse.chi, James.adam.anderson, Jerryobject, Jreast, JustAnotherJoe, Linas, LostVagabond, Mdd, Nasa-verve, Nhumfrey, Nicolas1981, Opoirel, PRB, Pholding, ProfessorBaltasar, Pumba lt, R'n'B, Simnia, Soumyasch, Spencerk, Wbeaureg, White gecko, WiseWoman, 32 anonymous edits

Relational_database *Source*: http://en.wikipedia.org/w/index.php?title=Relational_database *Contributors*: *Kat*, 01001, 127, 217.162.105.xxx, 64.192.12.xxx, Abolen, Adamcscott, Adamrush, Admrboltz, Agateller, Ahoerstemeier, Alain Amiouni, Alansohn, Andre Engels, Angela, Anuja297, Appzter, Astheg, AutumnSnow, Banes, Beland, Beno1000, Bitnine, Bobo2000, Boothy443, Booyabazooka, Bpalitaa, Brick Thrower, Bsdlogical, CALR, Calmer Waters, Calvernaz, Chris.Giles, Chrislk02, Conversion script, Craig Stuntz, Cww, DARTH SIDIOUS 2, DVdm, Dandv, Danim, Dannydaman9, Darth Mike, Dave6, David Delony, Dfeuer, DinosaursLoveExistence, Dionyziz, Dirk P Broer, Drgs100, Dschwart11, Dumbledad, EagleFan, Eik Corell, El C, ElKevbo, Emperorbma, Fabrictramp(public), FatalError, FayssalF, Ferkelparade, Fidimayor, Fieldday-sunday, Filiocht, Findling67, FlyingDoctor, Francs2000, Fratrep, Fred Bradstadt, Freediving-beava, Frigotoni, Fuddle, Gaur1982, Gerbrant, Giftlite, Glane23, GoingBatty, Graham87, HJ Mitchell, Hapsiainen, Harold f, Herostratus, Hmrox, Hp-NJITWILL, I do not exist, ILikeBeer, IRP, Ideogram, Iohannes Animosus, J.delanoy, JCLately, JLaTondre, JaGa, Jacobrothstein, Jan Hidders, Jitendraapi, Jncraton, John Vandenberg, Johnuniq, Jon Awbrey, Jwoodger, Jóna Þórunn, K faiad, KingsleyIdehen, Klausness, KnowledgeOfSelf, Kostmo, Kraron, Kristensson, Krogstadt, Kuru, Larsinio, Leandrod, Lfstevens, Linlasj, Logthis, Looxix, Luna Santin, MC MasterChef, MER-C, Mac, MainlyDigGrammar, Mandarax, Manop, Mark Renier, Mark T, Mav, Mckaysalisbury, Merlion444, Metroking, Michael Hardy, Michael Hodgson, Mikeblas, MilerWhite, Mindmatrix, Msikma, NHRHS2010, Nannahara, Nanshu, Nisantha04, Niteowlneils, Nocohen, Ns.code, Odie5533, Olinga, Oursinees324, OwenBlacker, Oxymoron83, Pablo323, Pdcook, Pearle, Philcha, Pietdesomere, Pinkadelica, Psb777, Psychcf, Quitchy, Rasmus Faber, RayGates, Rchertzy, Rfl, Romanm, Rrburke, SandyGeorgia, Scouser0phil, Sequologist, Sfe1, Sgiovannini, Shinju, Sir Nicholas de Mimsy-Porpington, Sir Vicious, Slightlyusefulcat, Smjg, Solipsist, Sonett72, Specialbrad, Spiritia, Spudtater, SqlPac, Stare at the sun, SteinbDJ, Steve Casburn, Supten, TJRC, Tcncv, Tcnuk, Ted Longstaffe, Teles, TheDJ, Thingg, Tobias Bergemann, Todd Vredevoogd, Tom harrison, Triddle, Triwbe, Troels Arvin, Turnstep, Utcursch, Vespristiano, Wesley, Wolfraem, Wolfsbane2k, Xiong, Xphile2868, Zahid Abdassabur, Zipircik, 502 anonymous edits

AllegroGraph *Source*: http://en.wikipedia.org/w/index.php?title=AllegroGraph *Contributors*: Bruce Esrig, Ceran, Cnorvell, Cobaltbluetony, Danim, E40, Hairhorn, JLaTondre, OlEnglish, Paradoja, RadioFan, SamJohnston, Shimeru, Simeon, Stassats, 4 anonymous edits

Image Sources, Licenses and Contributors

GNU Free Documentation License Version 1.2, November 2002 Copyright (C) 2000,2001,2002 Free Software Foundation, Inc. 59 Temple Place, Suite 330, Boston, MA 02111-1307 USA Everyone is permitted to copy and distribute verbatim copies of this license document, but changing it is not allowed.

0. PREAMBLE
The purpose of this License is to make a manual, textbook, or other functional and useful document "free" in the sense of freedom: to assure everyone the effective freedom to copy and redistribute it, with or without modifying it, either commercially or noncommercially. Secondarily, this License preserves for the author and publisher a way to get credit for their work, while not being considered responsible for modifications made by others. This License is a kind of "copyleft", which means that derivative works of the document must themselves be free in the same sense. It complements the GNU General Public License, which is a copyleft license designed for free software. We have designed this License in order to use it for manuals for free software, because free software needs free documentation: a free program should come with manuals providing the same freedoms that the software does. But this License is not limited to software manuals; it can be used for any textual work, regardless of subject matter or whether it is published as a printed book. We recommend this License principally for works whose purpose is instruction or reference.

1. APPLICABILITY AND DEFINITIONS
This License applies to any manual or other work, in any medium, that contains a notice placed by the copyright holder saying it can be distributed under the terms of this License. Such a notice grants a world-wide, royalty-free license, unlimited in duration, to use that work under the conditions stated herein. The "Document", below, refers to any such manual or work. Any member of the public is a licensee, and is addressed as "you". You accept the license if you copy, modify or distribute the work in a way requiring permission under copyright law. A "Modified Version" of the Document means any work containing the Document or a portion of it, either copied verbatim, or with modifications and/or translated into another language. A "Secondary Section" is a named appendix or a front-matter section of the Document that deals exclusively with the relationship of the publishers or authors of the Document to the Document's overall subject (or to related matters) and contains nothing that could fall directly within that overall subject. (Thus, if the Document is in part a textbook of mathematics, a Secondary Section may not explain any mathematics.) The relationship could be a matter of historical connection with the subject or with related matters, or of legal, commercial, philosophical, ethical or political position regarding them. The "Invariant Sections" are certain Secondary Sections whose titles are designated, as being those of Invariant Sections, in the notice that says that the Document is released under this License. If a section does not fit the above definition of Secondary then it is not allowed to be designated as Invariant. The Document may contain zero Invariant Sections. If the Document does not identify any Invariant Sections then there are none. The "Cover Texts" are certain short passages of text that are listed, as Front-Cover Texts or Back-Cover Texts, in the notice that says that the Document is released under this License. A Front-Cover Text may be at most 5 words, and a Back-Cover Text may be at most 25 words. A "Transparent" copy of the Document means a machine-readable copy, represented in a format whose specification is available to the general public, that is suitable for revising the document straightforwardly with generic text editors or (for images composed of pixels) generic paint programs or (for drawings) some widely available drawing editor, and that is suitable for input to text formatters or for automatic translation to a variety of formats suitable for input to text formatters. A copy made in an otherwise Transparent file format whose markup, or absence of markup, has been arranged to thwart or discourage subsequent modification by readers is not Transparent. An image format is not Transparent if used for any substantial amount of text. A copy that is not "Transparent" is called "Opaque". Examples of suitable formats for Transparent copies include plain ASCII without markup, Texinfo input format, LaTeX input format, SGML or XML using a publicly available DTD, and standard-conforming simple HTML, PostScript or PDF designed for human modification. Examples of transparent image formats include PNG, XCF and JPG. Opaque formats include proprietary formats that can be read and edited only by proprietary word processors, SGML or XML for which the DTD and/or processing tools are not generally available, and the machine-generated HTML, PostScript or PDF produced by some word processors for output purposes only. The "Title Page" means, for a printed book, the title page itself, plus such following pages as are needed to hold, legibly, the material this License requires to appear in the title page. For works in formats which do not have any title page as such, "Title Page" means the text near the most prominent appearance of the work's title, preceding the beginning of the body of the text. A section "Entitled XYZ" means a named subunit of the Document whose title either is precisely XYZ or contains XYZ in parentheses following text that translates XYZ in another language. (Here XYZ stands for a specific section name mentioned below, such as "Acknowledgements", "Dedications", "Endorsements", or "History".) To "Preserve the Title" of such a section when you modify the Document means that it remains a section "Entitled XYZ" according to this definition. The Document may include Warranty Disclaimers next to the notice which states that this License applies to the Document. These Warranty Disclaimers are considered to be included by reference in this License, but only as regards disclaiming warranties: any other implication that these Warranty Disclaimers may have is void and has no effect on the meaning of this License.

2. VERBATIM COPYING
You may copy and distribute the Document in any medium, either commercially or noncommercially, provided that this License, the copyright notices, and the license notice saying this License applies to the Document are reproduced in all copies, and that you add no other conditions whatsoever to those of this License. You may not use technical measures to obstruct or control the reading or further copying of the copies you make or distribute. However, you may accept compensation in exchange for copies. If you distribute a large enough number of copies you must also follow the conditions in section 3. You may also lend copies, under the same conditions stated above, and you may publicly display copies.

3. COPYING IN QUANTITY
If you publish printed copies (or copies in media that commonly have printed covers) of the Document, numbering more than 100, and the Document's license notice requires Cover Texts, you must enclose the copies in covers that carry, clearly and legibly, all these Cover Texts: Front-Cover Texts on the front cover, and Back-Cover Texts on the back cover. Both covers must also clearly and legibly identify you as the publisher of these copies. The front cover must present the full title with all words of the title equally prominent and visible. You may add other material on the covers in addition. Copying with changes limited to the covers, as long as they preserve the title of the Document and satisfy these conditions, can be treated as verbatim copying in other respects. If the required texts for either cover are too voluminous to fit legibly, you should put the first ones listed (as many as fit reasonably) on the actual cover, and continue the rest onto adjacent pages. If you publish or distribute Opaque copies of the Document numbering more than 100, you must either include a machine-readable Transparent copy along with each Opaque copy, or state in or with each Opaque copy a computer-network location from which the general network-using public has access to download using public-standard network protocols a complete Transparent copy of the Document, free of added material. If you use the latter option, you must take reasonably prudent steps, when you begin distribution of Opaque copies in quantity, to ensure that this Transparent copy will remain thus accessible at the stated location until at least one year after the last time you distribute an Opaque copy (directly or through your agents or retailers) of that edition to the public. It is requested, but not required, that you contact the authors of the Document well before redistributing any large number of copies, to give them a chance to provide you with an updated version of the Document.

4. MODIFICATIONS
You may copy and distribute a Modified Version of the Document under the conditions of sections 2 and 3 above, provided that you release the Modified Version under precisely this License, with the Modified Version filling the role of the Document, thus licensing distribution and modification of the Modified Version to whoever possesses a copy of it. In addition, you must do these things in the Modified Version: A. Use in the Title Page (and on the covers, if any) a title distinct from that of the Document, and from those of previous versions (which should, if there were any, be listed in the History section of the Document). You may use the same title as a previous version if the original publisher of that version gives permission. B. List on the Title Page, as authors, one or more persons or entities responsible for authorship of the modifications in the Modified Version, together with at least five of the principal authors of the Document (all of its principal authors, if it has fewer than five), unless they release you from this requirement. C. State on the Title page the name of the publisher of the Modified Version, as the publisher. D. Preserve all the copyright notices of the Document. E. Add an appropriate copyright notice for your modifications adjacent to the other copyright notices. F. Include, immediately after the copyright notices, a license notice giving the public permission to use the Modified Version under the terms of this License, in the form shown in the Addendum below. G. Preserve in that license notice the full lists of Invariant Sections and required Cover Texts given in the Document's license notice. H. Include an unaltered copy of this License. I. Preserve the section Entitled "History", Preserve its Title, and add to it an item stating at least the title, year, new authors, and publisher of the Modified Version as given on the Title Page. If there is no section Entitled "History" in the Document, create one stating the title, year, authors, and publisher of the Document as given on its Title Page, then add an item describing the Modified Version as stated in the previous sentence. J. Preserve the network location, if any, given in the Document for public access to a Transparent copy of the Document, and likewise the network locations given in the Document for previous versions it was based on. These may be placed in the "History" section. You may omit a network location for a work that was published at least four years before the Document itself, or if the original publisher of the version it refers to gives permission. K. For any section Entitled "Acknowledgements" or "Dedications", Preserve the Title of the section, and preserve in the section all the substance and tone of each of the contributor acknowledgements and/or dedications given therein. L. Preserve all the Invariant Sections of the Document, unaltered in their text and in their titles. Section numbers or the equivalent are not considered part of the section titles. M. Delete any section Entitled "Endorsements". Such a section may not be included in the Modified Version. N. Do not retitle any existing section to be Entitled "Endorsements" or to conflict in title with any Invariant Section. O. Preserve any Warranty Disclaimers. If the Modified Version includes new front-matter sections or appendices that qualify as Secondary Sections and contain no material copied from the Document, you may at your option designate some or all of these sections as invariant. To do this, add their titles to the list of Invariant Sections in the Modified Version's license notice. These titles must be distinct from any other section titles. You may add a section Entitled "Endorsements", provided it contains nothing but endorsements of your Modified Version by various parties--for example, statements of peer review or that the text has been approved by an organization as the authoritative definition of a standard. You may add a passage of up to five words as a Front-Cover Text, and a passage of up to 25 words as a Back-Cover Text, to the end of the list of Cover Texts in the Modified Version. Only one passage of Front-Cover Text and one of Back-Cover Text may be added by (or through arrangements made by) any one entity. If the Document already includes a cover text for the same cover, previously added by you or by arrangement made by the same entity you are acting on behalf of, you may not add another; but you may replace the old one, on explicit permission from the previous publisher that added the old one. The author(s) and publisher(s) of the Document do not by this License give permission to use their names for publicity for or to assert or imply endorsement of any Modified Version.

5. COMBINING DOCUMENTS
You may combine the Document with other documents released under this License, under the terms defined in section 4 above for modified versions, provided that you include in the combination all of the Invariant Sections of all of the original documents, unmodified, and list them all as Invariant Sections of your combined work in its license notice, and that you preserve all their Warranty Disclaimers. The combined work need only contain one copy of this License, and multiple identical Invariant Sections may be replaced with a single copy. If there are multiple Invariant Sections with the same name but different contents, make the title of each such section unique by adding at the end of it, in parentheses, the name of the original author or publisher of that section if known, or else a unique number. Make the same adjustment to the section titles in the list of Invariant Sections in the license notice of the combined work. In the combination, you must combine any sections Entitled "History" in the various original documents, forming one section Entitled "History"; likewise combine any sections Entitled "Acknowledgements", and any sections Entitled "Dedications". You must delete all sections Entitled "Endorsements".

6. COLLECTIONS OF DOCUMENTS
You may make a collection consisting of the Document and other documents released under this License, and replace the individual copies of this License in the various documents with a single copy that is included in the collection, provided that you follow the rules of this License for verbatim copying of each of the documents in all other respects. You may extract a single document from such a collection, and distribute it individually under this License, provided you insert a copy of this License into the extracted document, and follow this License in all other respects regarding verbatim copying of that document.

7. AGGREGATION WITH INDEPENDENT WORKS
A compilation of the Document or its derivatives with other separate and independent documents or works, in or on a volume of a storage or distribution medium, is called an "aggregate" if the copyright resulting from the compilation is not used to limit the legal rights of the compilation's users beyond what the individual works permit. When the Document is included in an aggregate, this License does not apply to the other works in the aggregate which are not themselves derivative works of the Document. If the Cover Text requirement of section 3 is applicable to these copies of the Document, then if the Document is less than one half of the entire aggregate, the Document's Cover Texts may be placed on covers that bracket the Document within the aggregate, or the electronic equivalent of covers if the Document is in electronic form. Otherwise they must appear on printed covers that bracket the whole aggregate.

8. TRANSLATION
Translation is considered a kind of modification, so you may distribute translations of the Document under the terms of section 4. Replacing Invariant Sections with translations requires special permission from their copyright holders, but you may include translations of some or all Invariant Sections in addition to the original versions of these Invariant Sections. You may include a translation of this License, and all the license notices in the Document, and any Warranty Disclaimers, provided that you also include the original English version of this License and the original versions of those notices and disclaimers. In case of a disagreement between the translation and the original version of this License or a notice or disclaimer, the original version will prevail. If a section in the Document is Entitled "Acknowledgements", "Dedications", or "History", the requirement (section 4) to Preserve its Title (section 1) will typically require changing the actual title.

9. TERMINATION
You may not copy, modify, sublicense, or distribute the Document except as expressly provided for under this License. Any other attempt to copy, modify, sublicense or distribute the Document is void, and will automatically terminate your rights under this License. However, parties who have received copies, or rights, from you under this License will not have their licenses terminated so long as such parties remain in full compliance.

10. FUTURE REVISIONS OF THIS LICENSE
The Free Software Foundation may publish new, revised versions of the GNU Free Documentation License from time to time. Such new versions will be similar in spirit to the present version, but may differ in detail to address new problems or concerns. See http://www.gnu.org/copyleft/. Each version of the License is given a distinguishing version number. If the Document specifies that a particular numbered version of this License "or any later version" applies to it, you have the option of following the terms and conditions either of that specified version or of any later version that has been published (not as a draft) by the Free Software Foundation. If the Document does not specify a version number of this License, you may choose any version ever published (not as a draft) by the Free Software Foundation. ADDENDUM: How to use this License for your documents To use this License in a document you have written, include a copy of the License in the document and put the following copyright and license notices just after the title page: Copyright (c) YEAR YOUR NAME. Permission is granted to copy, distribute and/or modify this document under the terms of the GNU Free Documentation License, Version 1.2 or any later version published by the Free Software Foundation; with no Invariant Sections, no Front-Cover Texts, and no Back-Cover Texts. A copy of the license is included in the section entitled "GNU Free Documentation License". If you have Invariant Sections, Front-Cover Texts and Back-Cover Texts, replace the "with...Texts." line with this: with the Invariant Sections being LIST THEIR TITLES, with the Front-Cover Texts being LIST, and with the Back-Cover Texts being LIST. If you have Invariant Sections without Cover Texts, or some other combination of the three, merge those two alternatives to suit the situation. If your document contains nontrivial examples of program code, we recommend releasing these examples in parallel under your choice of free software license, such as the GNU General Public License, to permit their use in free software.